BE A
SEQUOI
NOT A
BONSA

BE A

THE SEVEN GROWTH SECRETS

SEQUOIA

OF THE WORLD'S MOST

NOT A

SUCCESSFUL COMPANIES

BONSAI

NICOLAS DARVEAU-GARNEAU

FORMER GOOGLE CHIEF EVANGELIST

HarperCollins
Leadership

HarperCollins Publishers, Macken House, 39/40 Mayor Street Upper, Dublin 1, D01 C9W8, Ireland (https://www.harpercollins.com)

Library of Congress Control Number: 2025947499

Art direction: Ron Huizinga
Cover design: Faceout Studio / Tim Green
Interior Design: Neuwirth & Associates, Inc.

Printed in the United States of America
25 26 27 28 29 LBC 5 4 3 2 1

To the more than one thousand CEOs and CMOs I met during my years as Google's chief evangelist and to the dedicated Googlers who help them grow their business every day.

CONTENTS

INTRODUCTION

At the start of the pandemic, Invisalign faced a tough challenge as it relied on dentist offices, many of which were closed, to sell its braces. In contrast, its competitor, SmileDirectClub, sold directly to consumers and seemed poised to gain market share. Surprisingly, the opposite happened: Invisalign's sales grew 28 percent year-over-year in Q4 2020, surpassing Wall Street estimates by 43 percent. Profits rose 50 percent, and the company's market capitalization increased by over $7 billion.[1] In contrast, SmileDirectClub's sales fell 6 percent.[2] How could this happen?

Surex, an online car insurance broker, was struggling to grow profitably as car repair costs continued to rise. Due to regulatory constraints, it couldn't fully offset these costs by raising premiums. To restore profitable growth, the company radically changed its customer acquisition strategy. Within a year, it acquired 60 percent fewer customers in the highest-risk, least profitable segment and 90 percent more in the most profitable segment. This shift helped Surex quadruple its profits. How can a company improve the profitability of the new customers it acquires so dramatically, and so quickly?

The Asbury Automotive Group, a midsize car dealership group, was the first in North America to sell cars entirely online. Through Asbury's website, Clicklane.com, customers can complete a legally binding transaction to buy a car, trade in their current car at a guaranteed price, secure financing with real-time offers from multiple banks, and purchase supplemental insurance like tire and wheel coverage—all in under ten minutes.

By improving its customer experience, Asbury achieved impressive results over five years: a 30 percent increase in customer satisfaction,[3] 22 percent growth in revenues, and a 33 percent rise in profits.[4] These results are even more remarkable given that total car sales remained essentially flat[5] and competitors like AutoNation saw profits drop 10 percent.[6] How did Asbury, with its limited resources, achieve such success?

And how did St. Jude Children's Research Hospital, already a global leader raising over $1 billion annually, achieve a remarkable 46 percent increase in online donations in just one year to scale its mission of eradicating childhood cancer? Thanks to its continued fundraising success, St. Jude is now able to distribute free cancer drugs to sick children in sixty countries!

AS GOOGLE'S CHIEF evangelist and in my own growth consulting practice, I advised more than one thousand companies, including several that I reference in this book, and have seen firsthand how a select few consistently grow profits faster and more sustainably than competitors. In this book, I will reveal their secrets.[7]

The practical ideas you will learn from the hundreds of examples and case studies will help you profitably outgrow your competitors, even if your company doesn't have better products,[8] lower costs, or a recognized brand. These profit-maximizing ideas have worked for many companies in different industries, can be executed by companies of all sizes, and can be tested inexpensively. What's more, these ideas don't rely on risky acquisitions, hit-and-miss new product development, or expensive technology investments. All you need is the willingness to think differently and try new things.

As Rick Shadyac, president and CEO of ALSAC, the fundraising and awareness organization for St. Jude Children's Research Hospital, from 2009 to 2025, explained in our interview, "One of the reasons we've been successful is that, after a meeting with Google's evangelists in Mountain

View—one of the most important meetings of my career—we challenged what you called our 'rivers of thinking,' our ability to go beyond the current flow of our ideas. In the end, what made the difference was that we thought differently."

ON SEQUOIAS AND BONSAI

Sequoias are the tallest trees on Earth, growing more than three hundred feet high. They are not perfect—their trunks split easily, and branches grow haphazardly—but they continue to grow. Surprisingly, they grow faster as they get older and capture more sunlight above the forest canopy.

At the other end of the spectrum is the bonsai. These trees, continuously pruned to perfection, look spectacular. But they remain small, and their lifespan is only a tenth of a sequoia's.

The contrast between sequoias and bonsai is a good metaphor for a company's strategy. Some companies continually prune, focusing mainly on short-term efficiency and perfection. Others maximize sustainable, longer-term profitable growth, even if everything isn't perfect in the very short term.

SEVEN DIFFERENCES BETWEEN SEQUOIAS AND BONSAI

Since leaving Google, I've reflected on the more than one thousand meetings I had with C-suite executives from around the world. These leaders visited the Partner Plex, Google's state-of-the-art venue showcasing the latest advances in AI. We would begin each day in front of a giant screen displaying interesting insights about their business, including live customer feedback from across the globe, a visual that never failed to captivate CEOs.

My team of dedicated Google evangelists worked closely with these executives to refine their profitable growth strategies. With the benefit of hindsight, I've identified seven key differences between the companies that thrived in the years following our meetings (the sequoias) and those that struggled to grow profitably (the bonsai).

1. **Maximize profitable growth:** Bonsai focus on efficiency metrics. In marketing, they use metrics like customer acquisition cost (CAC) or return on ad spend (ROAS),[9] while sequoias focus on maximum profits. And, as I discovered, if a company's marketing team is focused on efficiency, chances are high that the rest of the company is too.

   In chapter 1, we cover how to change your metrics, dashboards, and mindsets to maximize profitable growth. We will also cover how to transition from an efficiency-focused bonsai strategy to a profit-maximizing sequoia strategy with minimal risk.

2. **Focus on the longer-term:** While bonsai focus mostly on the short term, sequoias focus intensely on the longer term and try to maximize metrics like customer lifetime value profits (CLV), the predicted future profit of each customer.

   In chapter 2, we cover how to use CLV to optimize your business and how to transition from a short-term optimization strategy to a longer-term CLV strategy with minimal risk.

3. **Acquire the most valuable customers:** Bonsai focus on acquiring as many customers as possible at the lowest possible CAC, while sequoias focus on acquiring as many high-CLV customers as possible. This focus on quality often results in substantially higher longer-term profits, especially in industries where a small percentage of customers generate most of the profits.

   In chapter 3, we cover how to forecast the CLV of each new customer, use that forecast to acquire more high-CLV customers, and test and scale this strategy quickly, inexpensively, and with minimal risk.

4. **Improve the CLV of existing customers:** Bonsai focus on improving financial metrics, while sequoias prioritize customer-focused metrics like CLV. By growing CLV faster, sequoias earn more per existing customer and can therefore invest more to acquire new ones. This creates a flywheel of sustained, profitable growth.

   In chapter 4, we cover how to forecast the CLV of individual existing customers and how to generate, test, and scale ideas to increase that CLV.

5. **Improve your brand profitably:** Bonsai cling to outdated branding strategies rooted in the days of television, which often fail to deliver results. Sequoias, on the other hand, adopt scientific, digital-first branding approaches that quickly improve brand metrics, leading to substantial gains in market share and profitability.

   In chapter 5, we cover how to predict the profitability of brand advertising in real time, leverage AI to personalize and target branding ads for high-CLV customers, and test and optimize branding campaigns to maximize results.

6. **Deliver an exceptional customer experience:** Sequoias focus on deeply understanding the needs of high-CLV customers. They deliver personalized, seamless experiences that attract more high-CLV customers and increase CLV over time. In contrast, bonsai design experiences for the average customer and prioritize short-term metrics like conversion rates.

   In chapter 6, we cover how to improve your customer experience, especially for high-CLV customers, with the lowest possible investment and risk.

7. **Evolve faster:** While the first six ideas are powerful, there are countless other ways to accelerate long-term profitable growth.

Sequoias stay ahead because they test and scale new ideas faster and more aggressively than bonsai.

In chapter 7, we cover how to build a world-class system for generating, testing, and implementing growth ideas quickly and cost-effectively. We also discuss how to continuously improve this system to maintain a competitive edge.

Imagine competing against a company that excels in these areas: It acquires the industry's most valuable customers, continually increases the CLV of its existing customers, delivers an unparalleled customer experience, strengthens its brand, and tests new ideas far faster than you.

If you implement the ideas in this book, you won't have to compete against this mighty sequoia. Instead, you'll become the sequoia all competitors fear.

BE A
SEQUOIA
NOT A
BONSAI

1

MAXIMIZE
PROFITABLE GROWTH

The most important difference between sequoias and bonsai is their goal. In nature, sequoias are genetically programmed to grow tall; it's in their DNA. Staying small is not an option for a sequoia if it wants to survive, as larger sequoias will capture all the sunlight. By contrast, bonsai are ordinary trees (like cherry or maple) that stay small because they are pruned by humans to do so.

The same is true in business. Corporate sequoias prioritize profitable growth, while bonsai concentrate on efficiency. In my experience advising more than a thousand companies, I estimate that more than 95 percent of marketers focus on efficiency metrics like customer acquisition cost (CAC) and return on ad spend (ROAS) to optimize their advertising investment instead of trying to maximize profits.

Chris O'Neil, former head of Google Canada, agrees: "In my nine years at Google, I can count on one hand the number of companies who optimized profits. Almost all others were wrongly optimizing efficiency metrics like ROAS and cost per lead instead, a big mistake." Chris is now CEO of GrowthLoop, an innovative data and AI company. "We're working with some of the best marketers in the world like Google, Priceline, and Indeed. They leverage unique customer insights and AI to increase CLV. Companies who focus on CLV, not short-term efficiency, are much more likely to win over time."

Seth van der Swaagh, managing director of Google's financial practice and a twenty-one-year Google veteran known for driving successful digital transformations, shared a similar perspective: "Many of my clients still focus on efficiency metrics rather than profitable growth metrics. My team works hard to change their approach, but it's challenging because we need to convince the heads of the business unit, the CMO, and the CFO before a company changes its KPIs. It's a big shift in mindset."

Optimizing the wrong key performance indicator (KPI) has always been problematic, but in the age of AI, it can be catastrophic. Advanced AI algorithms can quickly accelerate a company off course when given the wrong objectives.

Marketing is often just the canary in the coal mine. In my experience, if the marketing team prioritizes efficiency over profitable growth, it's likely that the rest of the company does too.

ST. JUDE INCREASES ONLINE
DONATIONS BY 46 PERCENT IN ONE YEAR

St. Jude Children's Research Hospital, a world-renowned cancer hospital, treats more than eight thousand children a year, at no cost to the families. St. Jude donors pay for everything: treatment for the sick child and housing, food, and transportation for the immediate family.

St. Jude also does a significant percentage of the worldwide research on childhood cancers and has been a key contributor in increasing the five-year survival rate in the US from 20 percent in 1962 to 80 percent today. Unfortunately, children living in certain parts of the world face much worse odds. In low- and even middle-income countries, the five-year survival rate for childhood cancer is still around 20 percent. In fact, the number one predictor of childhood cancer survival is where a child lives.[1] This is why St. Jude works with more than four hundred childhood cancer organizations worldwide to help them provide better treatment and family services. It trains health care professionals, provides technology, and shares all its research.

Doing this extraordinary work costs more than $2 billion annually. Eighty-nine percent of St. Jude's funds come from public donations—compared to less than 10 percent for most other hospitals. Remarkably, 80 percent of St. Jude's funding comes from eleven million active small donors who primarily donate online. Over the last fifteen years, St. Jude's fundraising arm, ALSAC, has quadrupled donations, growing them every quarter for sixty quarters in a row. St. Jude has become so good at online fundraising that it launched an academy to help other charities improve their efforts.

Yet, in 2020, St. Jude outdid itself, increasing online donations by an astounding 46 percent, raising hundreds of millions more in a single year.[2]

St. Jude's rapid donation growth was driven in part by its shift to a growth-oriented KPI to optimize its Google advertising strategy. As Nick Meads, a dedicated Googler who has advised St. Jude for years, says, "One of the most important things they did was focus on the results that mattered most to them, like donors engaged and donations raised, rather than an inflexible ROAS target. St. Jude has always been willing to test new ideas to see what has the biggest impact."

This additional fundraising will help fulfill the powerful vision Rick Shadyac shared: "We want to help as many children as possible and, through our research efforts, eradicate childhood cancer worldwide. One of our key goals now is to raise the childhood cancer survival rate from 20 percent to 60 percent in low- and middle-income countries. When the mission is that important, you remain open to new and innovative ways of fundraising. We're also fortunate to have a board that allows us to invest in growth ideas when the right opportunities arise."

WHY ARE SO MANY
COMPANIES FOCUSED ON EFFICIENCY?

If changing a marketing KPI can dramatically improve results, why are so few companies optimizing growth metrics like profits instead of efficiency metrics like ROAS? There are three main reasons:

1. **ROAS is the standard:** While this has started to change recently, advertising platforms like Google, Facebook, and Instagram have long prioritized ROAS as the primary KPI in their dashboards. As a result, most company advertising dashboards still rely on ROAS as their main KPI. Almost all marketing books, articles, and case studies, even today, focus on ROAS.

   ChatGPT defines performance advertising as "Advertising . . . whose primary goal is to achieve immediate and quantifiable results, often tied to metrics like return on ad spend (ROAS) or cost per acquisition (CPA)."[3] Not to be outdone, Google's own large language model, Gemini, defines performance advertising as "To drive immediate, measurable actions from consumers, such as clicks, leads, sales, or downloads. It's all about generating a quick return on investment (ROI)."[4]

2. **It was hard to optimize profits before:** Until recently, there was no easy way to automatically optimize advertising campaigns for profits. For instance, until a few years ago, Google's most advanced AI optimization tool was "Target ROAS," which maximized the ROAS of an advertising investment, not its profits. Digital advertising platforms like Google now offer advanced tools that automatically optimize for profit.

3. **Advertising is seen as a spend:** For many companies, the finance team still sees advertising as a spend that needs to be cut, not an investment that needs to be grown. The root cause

is a failure by marketing and finance to agree on the impact of advertising.

While it seems hard to believe that a very small percentage of marketing teams try to maximize profits, chances are that your marketing team is making the same mistake. To find out, ask the person managing your digital advertising investments (someone with a title like manager of Google Ads or director of performance marketing) what KPI they prioritize. I would bet you a lot that it has nothing to do with profits.

And if the marketing team, the place where profit maximization should be a given, isn't focused on maximizing profit, what are the chances that other teams, such as product development, customer service, procurement, or sales, are doing so? Not very high.

The good news is that you don't need to invest a lot of money to change your company's focus from efficiency to profitable growth. You just need to change your mindset.

Of course, there may be times when choosing a metric other than profits seems to make sense, like focusing on growing market share to beat a competitor in a new market. In chapter 2, we will cover how you can gain significant market share and maximize profits at the same time.

A FIVE-STEP PROCESS
TO SIGNIFICANTLY IMPROVE PROFITS

Many companies have successfully transitioned from a focus on efficiency to profit optimization. In my second role at Google, I led a team that worked with more than four hundred performance advertisers. During our initial meeting, we asked each company to define what success would look like in a year. Nearly all indicated that their main goal was to increase ROAS.

Within a year, we had worked with the great majority of these companies to track the daily profits of their Google advertising investment. We also convinced many of them to change their KPI from ROAS to maximum profits. Many of the companies who made that change and followed the subsequent steps increased the profits of their Google investment significantly and quickly.

Some examples of companies that changed their KPI from efficiency to growth include EverQuote, who increased profits by 170 percent,[5] and Autobytel who increased profits by 60 percent.[6]

The following is a low-risk and cost-effective five-step process to help your company shift its focus from efficiency to profit optimization. We'll first cover how to implement this approach in the marketing team, often the easiest and most impactful area to optimize. We'll then cover how to extend this transformation to other departments, turning them into profit-maximizing sequoias as well.

STEP 1—MAKE PROFITS YOUR MAIN MARKETING KPI

Which of these two charities is doing better, Charity A, which raises two dollars for every one dollar it invests in paid advertising, or Charity B, which raises five dollars for every one dollar? Most marketers would choose Charity B because it has a higher ROAS (5:1). But it's a trick question: There's not enough information to choose between Charities A and B.

Which charity is doing better now that you can see the information in figure 1.1, which shows that Charity A invested $10 million to raise $20 million in donations and Charity B invested $1 million to raise $5 million in donations?

FIGURE 1.1 ADVERTISING RESULTS FOR TWO CHARITIES

Charity	Advertising Investment	Donations	Net Donations
A	$10M	$20M	$10M
B	$1M	$5M	$4M

Hopefully, it should be obvious that Charity A is better. It raised $20 million for an advertising investment of $10 million. While its ROAS is a meager 2:1, it raised $10 million of net donations, the donations left after paying for the advertising investment. Charity B, on the other hand, raised $5 million on an advertising investment of $1 million for an impressive 5:1 ROAS but only $4 million of net donations.

The simple dashboard in figure 1.2 is a good way to summarize Charity A's strategy. It tracks net donations monthly and compares them to the previous year. A dashboard like this would encourage the marketing team to maximize net donations and to beat last year's results by as much as possible.

FIGURE 1.2 A GREAT ADVERTISING DASHBOARD
NET DONATIONS FROM ONLINE ADVERTISING

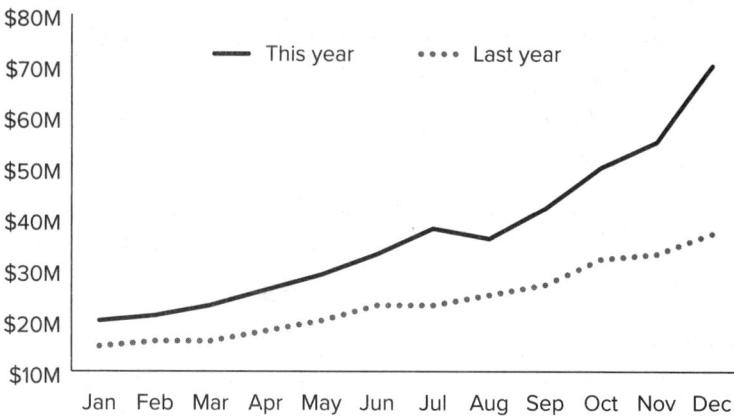

Charity B's dashboard, on the other hand, would look like the one in figure 1.3 below. I've seen hundreds of similar dashboards in many industries. In fact, this was the dashboard I wrongly used for years when I was an entrepreneur.

FIGURE 1.3 A TYPICAL ADVERTISING DASHBOARD

	Donations	Advertising Spend	ROAS
Jan	$1M	$0.5M	2:1
Feb	$2M	$0.5M	4:1
Mar	$3M	$0.5M	6:1
Apr	$3M	$0.5M	6:1
May	$3M	$0.5M	6:1

At first glance Charity B seems to be doing great. It tripled donations in just three months while keeping its advertising investment constant. As a result, its ROAS increased from 2:1 to 6:1. What's not to like?

First, this dashboard does not challenge the fundraising team to maximize net donations. Could Charity B raise significantly more net donations by increasing its advertising investment to $5 million next month, compared to its current $0.5 million? With this dashboard, Charity B will probably never try it.

Second, since ROAS is the primary metric in the dashboard, the marketing team naturally focuses on improving it. It's human nature to want dashboard numbers to go up. As a result, the team will prioritize efficiency over maximizing net donations. This approach will inevitably cause net donations to plateau, which already appears to be happening.

Third, this dashboard calls advertising a spend instead of an investment. This subtle difference almost always creates a mindset of efficiency, not growth.

In my experience, Charity B will feel great about its fundraising strategy, unaware of the significant opportunity it's probably missing.

I've encountered many companies that didn't realize they could greatly increase advertising profits until it was brought to their attention. Those that shifted their strategy toward maximizing profitable growth almost always saw substantial profit increases.

If you decide to shift your KPI from efficiency to profitable growth, it's important that the new profit metric be clear, complete, and consistent.

Clear

The charity fundraising example shown previously is simple: Cash invested in advertising generates cash donations, with few other costs to worry about. Most businesses are obviously far more complex and need to account for margins, customer service costs, returns, and many other costs.

This added complexity often leads to confusion. For instance, in my post-Google consulting work, I advised an airline who wanted to lower their advertising investment because the CMO thought it was unprofitable. After a discussion with the CMO and the CFO, we agreed that their $10 million monthly investment resulted in $50 million of incremental bookings, but we disagreed on how much profit that generated. (Note: While these numbers are directionally correct, I have changed them to hide the company's identity. I will use this approach for all anonymous case studies in this book.)

My view was that nearly all of that $50 million in bookings would fall to the bottom line as adding one more passenger to a flight that's not full adds minimal cost (credit card fees and a small increase in fuel consumption, baggage handling, and meal costs). My math showed that the $10 million investment generated approximately $35 million of profits after the advertising investment.[7] The CFO added other operating costs like maintenance and plane depreciation, lowering the profitability of the marketing investment to $20 million. The CMO added yet other costs, like insurance and part of the staff at headquarters, making the investment unprofitable.

The airline eventually settled on a profit formula that was somewhere between the CFO's definition and mine. Over the next year, the airline significantly increased the profitability of its advertising investment.

Complete

In addition to being clear, a profit formula should be complete and reflect a company's full profitability. I advised many retailers that increased the profits of their advertising investment by switching from a ROAS KPI to a maximizing profit KPI. But their initial definition of profit was sometimes basic: the revenues generated by advertising multiplied by their average gross margin minus the advertising investment. Over time, many of these retailers improved this definition by:

- **Adding more granular margin data:** By adding transaction-level margin, AI advertising systems like Google's will likely increase a retailer's profits.[8] But since most retailers do not have product-level gross margin data, we often started with an estimate of the gross margin of each transaction based on the category of the goods purchased. In my experience, this simple modification often generated more than 25 percent additional profit. Adding more accurate product-level margin data typically increased profits by another 15 percent.

- **Adding the full costs:** We would then add a retailer's full costs into the profit calculation since every transaction has credit card, shipping and handling, and sometimes return costs.[9] This additional data often increased profits by another 15 percent.

- **Adding store sales:** Since many customers research online before they buy in-store, we worked with retailers to add the store sales influenced by advertising. This enabled the advertising AI tools to optimize omnichannel profits, not just e-commerce profits. This change often dramatically increased profits.

Pandora, the world's largest jewelry retailer, followed a similar strategy. The impact was a staggering 200 percent increase in store revenues and 77 percent increase in total revenues driven by Google advertising.[10] There's no profit data in the case study, but it's likely substantial.

In total, many retailers more than doubled the profits of their advertising investment by simply changing the definition of profits. If you're concerned about sharing sensitive profit data with your advertising platform partners, just index it.

Consistent

Once the profit metric is clear and complete, it's important it stays consistent. In my experience, even great marketers tend to seesaw between profit maximization and efficiency.

A Fortune 500 company recently posted a job opening for a "head of growth." The job description outlined two key objectives: increase profits (yes!) and lower CAC (no!). A head of growth attempting to optimize both simultaneously will face constant challenges. One week, the focus might be on lowering CAC, which will likely hinder growth. The following week, after a frantic call from the finance team about missing monthly revenue targets, the focus will shift back to growth. This will likely increase CAC, and the cycle will continue. I did this way too often when I was an entrepreneur.

The solution to this tension between revenue growth and efficiency is to keep the focus on profits, a single metric that balances the trade-off between the two.

It's also important to stay disciplined. If the numbers in a profit dashboard, like the one in figure 1.2, are improving, why ask questions like, "Why is our advertising spend so high this month?" or "Why is our

CAC increasing?" The advertising spend (investment, please) and the CAC are irrelevant. All that matters is that profits are growing. Even a single question like that from an executive can turn a growing sequoia into a bonsai. I made that mistake as an entrepreneur too.

When building a profit dashboard, it's crucial to ensure profits aren't increased at the expense of customer satisfaction. To prevent this problem, include a customer satisfaction metric as a "guardrail measure." We will cover this issue in later chapters.

STEP 2—FULLY MAXIMIZE PROFITABLE GROWTH

Sequoias don't impose artificial limitations on their growth; they strive to grow as tall and as fast as possible. Most sequoias I advised had a flexible advertising budget, adjusted at least daily, to maximize profits. If an additional dollar invested on advertising could generate more profit, these sequoias found a way to budget it.

As Nick Meads says, "The advertising budget of St. Jude was fluid and they aimed to invest more in advertising if the additional investment also increased net donations." As one of my Google colleagues liked to say to his clients who didn't have a flexible advertising budget: "Don't turn off the money printing machine to save on electricity."

Airbnb moved to a flexible advertising budget years ago. Maria Hwang, the online advertising manager at the time of that change, said, "We will spend as long as we can make a certain profit. We're not constrained by budget. Our leadership is focused on the business impact of our . . . investments and empowers us to find new ways to drive results." With this strategy, Airbnb acquired 101 percent more customers from its Google advertising investment in six months.[11]

Flexible budgets are not only for digital-first companies. Wyndham Hotels did the same thing, with the CMO and CFO working closely together, daily, to adjust advertising budgets.[12] And TAP Airlines, the

Portuguese airline, saw its North American sales rise 350 percent when it moved from a fixed advertising budget to a flexible budget.[13]

Seth van der Swaagh worked with a major bank that established a center of excellence for digital marketing. This center partners closely with the finance team and all business lines to adjust advertising budgets quickly in response to new opportunities. According to Seth, "The bank has significantly increased profits and market share over the last two years with this strategy. The impact has been astounding."

According to Marie Gurlin-Merle, former CMO of Calvin Klein and L'Oréal USA: "Budget-agile marketers are 25% more likely than non-agile marketers to report their performance as stronger than industry competitors. And 48% of budget-agile marketers state that their marketing performance exceeded internal expectations and marketing KPIs, compared to 33% of marketers who are not budget agile."[14]

But unfortunately, most marketers think they are much more agile than they really are. In fact, continues Gurlin-Merle, "On average, 60% of marketers who say they are 'extremely agile' only make budget adjustments across digital channels monthly or less frequently. While this gap between perception and actual behavior happens at all levels of an organization, C-level executives are 2X more likely than individual contributors to perceive their business as extremely budget agile."[15]

Another issue that sometimes makes it difficult to fully maximize profits is that they're split across a complex value chain. Hotel companies and their franchisees have very different economic incentives, which can lead to poor decisions. If a franchised hotel has a hundred empty rooms tonight from which they could make $30,000 in profit, it should be willing to invest a lot in advertising (in theory as much as $29,999) to fill these rooms. But since the hotel company, not the franchisee, is in charge of advertising, it will not invest a lot since it only gets a small percent of the hotel's revenues (around 8–14 percent). The result of this misalignment is a significant loss in profit for both.

The solution would be to prove that investing more in advertising can significantly increase the profits of a few test hotels and then renegotiate franchise agreements to better align incentives.

STEP 3—OPTIMIZE HOLISTICALLY

Sequoias don't care if a branch or two is growing imperfectly. They focus on the growth of the overall tree. On the other hand, bonsai get trimmed any time a branch shows any imperfection, at the expense of the tree's overall growth.

History is full of companies that optimized themselves into irrelevance. For example, Penn Central Railroad went bankrupt in 1970 because, in part, it optimized each route without considering the results for the overall network.

Figure 1.4 examines the profitability (not ROAS) of digital advertising channels for a fictitious company. In this scenario, if this company looks at each channel separately, it will see that Google Ads make $15 million, Amazon ads $10 million, and TikTok ads lose $1 million. Since most companies evaluate advertising at the individual channel level, many would cut their TikTok investment.

But because advertising channels reinforce one another, it's important to look at results holistically. In this example, the most profitable scenario, which generates $32 million in profit, is to invest in all three channels. In fact, if TikTok ads were cut, the remaining Google and Amazon ads would generate $28 million of profit, a 12.5 percent loss of profit.

The best way to ensure your marketing team focuses on maximizing overall profit, rather than individual channel profits, is by using a dashboard like the one in figure 1.2 that doesn't segment results by channel. While the team should still track channel-level data for day-to-day optimization, the dashboard should make it clear that the ultimate goal is total profits across all channels combined.

But since most advertising dashboards still look like the one in Figure 1.3, it's likely that your marketing team isn't approaching things this way.

FIGURE 1.4 HOLISTIC VERSUS ATOMISTIC THINKING

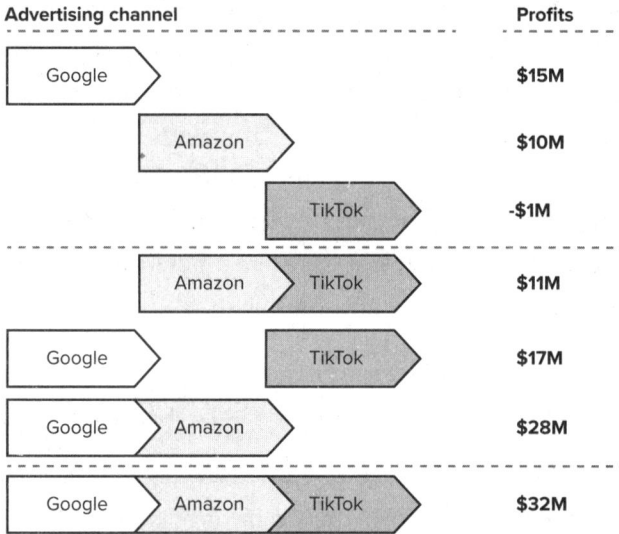

Advertising channel			Profits
Google			$15M
	Amazon		$10M
		TikTok	-$1M
	Amazon	TikTok	$11M
Google		TikTok	$17M
Google	Amazon		$28M
Google	Amazon	TikTok	$32M

I learned this lesson the hard way at one of my start-ups. We were investing more than $50,000 a day on digital advertising, and I was eager to find ways to prune. I asked our marketing team to identify tactics that had never directly led to acquiring a customer. To my surprise, we found that 30 percent of our advertising investment fell into this category. I immediately instructed the team to stop those tactics.

At first, the decision seemed brilliant—our customer acquisition numbers stayed strong while we saved 30 percent on advertising. But within two weeks, things unraveled. Customer acquisition plummeted by more than 40 percent, and even after reinstating the tactics we had cut, we never fully recovered.

Only in hindsight did I realize my mistake. Many of the tactics we cut weren't directly driving customer acquisitions but were playing an essential role in the customer journey. A customer might click on a banner ad but not buy immediately, then return days later through a search ad to complete the purchase. Our measurement system gave all the credit to the search ad, completely overlooking the banner ad's contribution.

Smarter advertisers, like Betterment, the fintech company, understand that advertising tactics work together, and they think holistically. For example, Betterment's YouTube campaigns were not profitable on their own, but they drove a 245 percent increase in searches for the Betterment brand. By optimizing YouTube ads and Google search ads together, Betterment was able to generate a significant increase in the profitability of its overall Google investment.[16]

STEP 4— PILOT AGGRESSIVELY, THEN SCALE

To transition from an efficiency-minded bonsai to a profit-maximizing sequoia, challenge your marketing team to maximize performance-advertising profits in a small market. To help them do that:

- **Build a profit dashboard:** Work with the marketing and finance teams to create an advertising profit dashboard, like the one in figure 1.2, with a clear and complete definition of profits. The dashboard should measure the overall profits of all advertising tactics holistically, not by individual tactics.

- **Maximize profits in a small market:** Encourage the marketing team to maximize profits in a small market (e.g., Idaho). If the team's focus has previously been efficiency, they'll need motivation to think bigger. Urge them to pursue every relevant advertising tactic aggressively across all major advertising platforms. While some wasted spending is inevitable, the initial goal is to be very aggressive. We'll cut the waste later. Since we're testing this idea in a small market, the waste will be relatively small anyway.

Consistently push for more profits in that market by asking questions like, "What can we do this week to increase total profits even more?" Then give the marketing team full autonomy to maximize profits. Don't get involved in tactics, and don't micromanage. Just evaluate the results in the dashboard with the team on a weekly basis.

Give the team as much budget as it needs to maximize profits. Since it's a small market, the additional budget will be small. If, for some reason, it's impossible to find additional budget, keep your current budget but invest the full amount required to maximize profits in the small test market by taking budget from other markets.

- **Trim the waste:** Once the team has developed the most aggressive, comprehensive, and profitable performance-advertising strategy possible in the small market, it's time to eliminate waste. If a specific advertising campaign appears very unprofitable, the team should remove it temporarily. If overall profits increase after the campaign is removed, it should be cut permanently. If profits decline, the campaign should be reinstated. While this method isn't highly scientific, it's quick and straightforward. The team should focus on cutting only tactics that seem clearly unprofitable, so precision isn't as critical for this process.

- **Scale:** Once the team has maximized profits in the small test market, the next step is to scale the advertising strategy to other markets. For a more cautious approach, expand gradually, rolling it out market by market at a pace that feels manageable and appropriate.

I call this the "Grow, Grow, Trim" strategy, and it consistently delivers remarkable results. The critical factor is unwavering support from senior management to cultivate a sequoia mindset within the marketing team, ensuring profits are thoroughly maximized in the test market before expanding to others.

STEP 5—USE THE SAME APPROACH OUTSIDE OF MARKETING

If marketing, the part of your company most clearly suited for profit optimization, isn't focused on maximizing profits, it's highly likely that other areas of your company aren't either. Let's examine a few departments.

Product Development

A software company measured the success of its product development team by the number of features launched. This led to a proliferation of features with questionable value. By shifting the focus to profit generated from product improvements, which the company could approximate based on usage, the development team began to better understand customer needs and prioritize features that customers were willing to pay for.

Atlassian, the team collaboration software company, shifted the focus of its product team away from adding features, toward delivering exceptional product experiences that effectively solve customer problems. As we will cover in chapter 4, helping customers achieve the results they want is one of the best ways to increase retention.[17]

Website and App Testing

Most website and app testing teams focus on one metric: conversion rate, the percentage of visitors who take an action like making a purchase, filling out a form, or downloading an app. As we'll discuss in chapters 6 and 7, however, conversion rate is a flawed metric. An e-commerce company could easily increase its conversion rate by offering unsustainable perks like deep discounts or free shipping for life, drastically reducing profits. A far better metric for website testing is profit per visitor.[18] I've seen a few companies adopt this approach with excellent results. Interestingly, after a few hours of research, I couldn't find a single public case study of a company doing it, indicating that very few companies do this—a big opportunity for those willing to try it.

Sales

B2B companies often evaluate their business development (BD) teams based on the number of sales-qualified leads (SQLs) they generate. But a BD team can inflate SQLs by targeting smaller, easier-to-qualify deals that add little profit. A more effective KPI measures the total profit the team contributes, factoring in both the number of SQLs and their profit potential as predicted by a lead scoring model. We will cover this topic in detail in chapter 2.

On average, B2B companies that deploy a lead scoring model increase revenues (and likely profits) by 18 percent.[19] TeamBuilding tripled its revenue (no word on profit) after using a lead scoring model.[20]

Customer Service

While it might seem logical to prioritize efficiency in customer service, focusing on metrics like average handle time (AHT) can cause significant issues. Initially, a focus on AHT can lead to cost savings, but often call volume surges as customers call back to get their issues fully resolved. Customer satisfaction can plummet and churn increase as rushed service and unresolved problems leave customers feeling undervalued.

Customer service teams should instead consider focusing on metrics like CSAT (customer satisfaction score), NPS (net promoter score), or FCR (first-call resolution) that reflect the quality of their customer service, while managing costs through better self-service and more advanced tools for agents.

In my post-Google consulting work, I worked with a company that measured the impact of customer service using a KPI called "profits saved," defined as the total profit retained from customers who avoided churning due to positive service experiences. This KPI motivated the customer service team to deliver better service while focusing on retaining the most profitable customers.

Procurement

Companies that prioritize cost reductions in their supply chains can face unintended consequences, such as reduced product quality, ethical violations, or safety risks. A more holistic procurement strategy considers factors like customer satisfaction, overall profitability, product quality, ethical sourcing, and environmental impact.

Britain's National Health Service (NHS) plans to invest in higher-quality incontinence pads. A pilot study showed that, while more expensive, the better-quality pads reduced leakage and required fewer changes, saving staff time and resources, potentially saving the NHS £520 million a year.[21]

Human Resources

Research shows that high-performing employees can be up to eight times more productive, and a third of executives cite finding top talent as their company's biggest challenge.[22] Despite this, many HR teams rely on metrics like time-to-hire or cost-per-hire, which rarely result in superstar hires. Similarly, metrics like employee engagement scores or employee NPS can drive positive overall changes but often fail to address the unique needs of high-performing employees.

PwC understands this. They segmented their employee survey by seniority and by employee performance and realized that, among their most senior consultants, the best performers were 15 percent more engaged than the average.[23]

By digging into the data using sophisticated software, PwC found that the main reasons for low engagement (and eventually attrition) among top-performing senior consultants changed with tenure, starting with dissatisfaction with diversity and inclusion efforts at first, to colleagues' lack of contributions later, and eventually to concerns about rewards and recognition after six years of tenure.

The data was also very different by gender. For example, 50 percent of high-performing female senior consultants were negative on equal pay compared to 39 percent for high-performing male senior consultants. Using this highly segmented data, PwC created a number of programs to increase the retention of high-performing senior consultants.

To turn all relevant departments of a company into profit-maximizing sequoias, I recommend you conduct a Profit Audit with each major department, which should include the following steps:

- **Learn the KPIs that drive behavior:** Identify the metrics that drive behaviors by interviewing frontline employees. While the official KPI for a logistics department might be the number of on-time deliveries, conversations with drivers could reveal they prioritize delivering as many packages as possible, regardless of timeliness. Even if their bonuses aren't tied to delivery volume, they may be rewarded with better routes for higher volume. This emphasis on speed could cause skipped quality checks and missed time slots for high-value deliveries, ultimately hurting profits.

- **Build a profit dashboard:** If the current KPIs don't maximize profits, collaborate with each department's leaders to create a profit-focused dashboard, which should include a clear, complete, and consistent definition of profits.

  A new dashboard for the logistics department could prioritize "profit per driver," a metric that combines the profit generated from on-time deliveries of packages with associated costs, such as fuel, vehicle depreciation, and maintenance. To create this dashboard, the company would assign a profit value and an expected delivery time for each package and credit drivers with the profit for each package delivered on time. Drivers would then plan their routes to maximize the on-time delivery of the most profitable packages. Over time, the logistics team could integrate advanced AI tools to further optimize route planning and package prioritization, continuously improving profitability.

- **Start a low-risk transition plan:** Work with the leadership of each department to design a low-risk transition plan to this new profit-centric approach. It would be unwise to roll out the strategy discussed above to all drivers immediately because it carries significant risks. What if drivers take much longer routes to prioritize delivering the most valuable packages, leading to substantial increases in fuel costs? What if valuable packages arrive on time, but the on-time delivery rates for other packages decline significantly?

  Instead, this new approach should be tested with a small group of drivers. This cautious strategy would allow the logistics department to refine the metrics and processes based on real-world feedback, ensuring increased profitability and customer satisfaction.

2

FOCUS ON
THE LONGER TERM

S equoias live up to three thousand years. One of the reasons for their longevity is that they plan, from their inception, to be around that long. To do so, they spend their first few years growing a root system that can extend a hundred feet in all directions, creating the right foundation for their future growth.

Corporate sequoias think the same way. While they of course care about what happens in the short term, they obsess over how to win in the longer term. In chapter 1, I discussed the importance of focusing on profitable growth, not ROAS or other efficiency metrics. In this chapter, I will share why you should focus on maximizing longer-term profits and why it will give you an advantage your competitors will struggle to match.

ONLINE RETAILERS DOUBLE PROFITS

I worked with many online retailers that switched their main advertising KPI from short-term profits to a longer-term profit KPI, defined as the predicted future profits from all customers minus the investment in advertising.

To implement this strategy, these retailers built two predictive models. The first model estimated a new customer's expected future profit by analyzing their buying behavior during the first few weeks after sign-up. This model was used in acquisition campaigns to target customers predicted to be much more profitable. In chapter 3, we will discuss how to build profit-prediction models for new customers and leverage them to acquire more profitable customers.

The second model predicted the future profitability for each existing customer by analyzing their entire purchase history. Based on these predictions, these retailers created a new segmentation strategy, dividing customers into deciles by forecasted profits and customizing promotions for each group. This strategy often led to a significant increase in the profitability of existing customers. In chapter 4, we'll explore how to build profit prediction models for existing customers and use them to increase their profitability.

In my experience, within less than a year, many of these retailers more than doubled their advertising profits.

WHY ARE SO MANY
COMPANIES SHORT-TERM FOCUSED?

Optimizing for long-term outcomes can deliver remarkable results, as the previous example demonstrated. Conversely, focusing solely on short-term profits can have disastrous consequences. In 1981, American Airlines introduced the AAirpass subscription for $400,000, allowing a customer and a companion to fly unlimited first-class trips for life. While it initially generated short-term cash flow, the long-term impact was costly. In 2007, when American Airlines evaluated individual customer profitability, they discovered their most loyal AAirpass customer,

Steven Rothstein, who had taken nearly ten thousand flights, had cost the company $23 million in lost profit.[1]

Another example is meal kit companies that deliver preportioned ingredients and recipes directly to consumers. While many of these companies grew rapidly, few became profitable, in part because they churned more than 90 percent of their subscribers within one year.[2] One of the reasons for this high churn was a focus on short-term KPIs. Most of these meal kit companies focused almost exclusively on the number of subscribers they acquired, not paying attention to the quality of these subscribers.

My former colleague Neil Hoyne, Google's chief strategist and author of *Converted*, a great book about data-driven tactics to win customers' hearts,[3] remains confused by this strategy: "We offered to help some of these companies build a churn-prediction model so they could acquire subscribers who would be much less likely to churn. But very few were interested. Almost all wanted to acquire new subscribers and didn't care how good those subscribers would be."

Despite the potential to significantly increase profits by switching to longer-term profit optimization, and the clear disadvantages of short-term-only profit optimization, very few companies optimize for the longer term. As a former Google colleague recently observed, "Although Google has published numerous case studies demonstrating the effectiveness of long-term profit optimization and developed powerful AI tools to help companies do it, none of the companies my team advises do it."

In fact, many companies don't even measure longer-term KPIs. For example, only 49 percent of B2B companies measure their retention rate and churn,[4] and only 25 percent of companies use predicted profits as a core marketing metric.[5]

In my experience, fewer than 1 percent of companies use long-term profits as their main KPI. Many factors contribute to the reluctance of almost all companies to optimize long-term profitability.

Fear of Hurting Short-Term Results

Some companies worry that focusing on longer-term profits will hurt their short-term results. In the case of meal kit companies, not adding new subscribers at a furious pace could have jeopardized their next round of venture capital, which they needed to stay in business in a highly competitive market.

But what if a meal kit company could attract fewer subscribers who churn quickly while acquiring more total subscribers? They could create a predictive model to flag new subscribers likely to churn right after the heavily discounted introductory period when meals are priced at 50–70 percent off. Using this data, AI advertising systems like Google's would optimize campaigns to try to avoid acquiring these highly unprofitable subscribers.

Let's assume a meal kit company loses $150 for every subscriber that churns after the promotional period: $100 to acquire the customers and $50 to send them a few weeks of food at 60 percent off. If the company could avoid acquiring ten thousand of these unprofitable subscribers, it would save $1.5 million, which it could reinvest to acquire fifteen thousand subscribers (for $100 each) that are more likely to stay beyond the promotional period and generate positive cash flow.

One way to avoid short-term-only thinking is by allocating resources based on timelines. In fact, companies who grow profits fastest are 70 percent more likely to have dedicated budgets for longer-term growth projects.[6] The CMO of a telecom company does it this way: "I assign 50 percent of resources to the first year, 30 percent to the second year, and 20 percent to year three. That means you don't keep falling off a cliff at the end of every year, and you build sustainable growth."[7]

Fear of Making Decisions with Imprecise Data

Some companies are more comfortable making decisions with accurate data (for example, the total number of subscribers acquired today) than making decisions with imprecise data (for example, the number of subscribers likely to stay after the promotional period). As a result, they often make bad decisions using perfect data.

This behavior is akin to an airline pilot flying without instruments, focusing on the precise outside temperature (–65.56° Fahrenheit) instead of focusing on the plane's approximate heading (350° plus or minus 20°).

It's surprising that companies struggle to make decisions with imprecise data because their executives do it all the time in their personal lives. Most executives would buy a $100 lottery ticket with a 30 percent chance of winning $1,000 in five years. Yet, at work, the same leaders sometimes shy away from similar bets because of psychological barriers like groupthink, loss aversion, and short-term rewards.[8]

The solution, as we will cover later, is to begin by using predictive models for low-risk decisions and gradually expand their application to higher-risk decisions over time.

Pressure from Stakeholders

Many companies face pressure from external stakeholders, such as shareholders and stock analysts, and internal stakeholders, like employees with quarterly bonuses, to deliver short-term results. These expectations can create an environment where leadership feels compelled to prioritize immediate gains over sustainable growth.

The solution is to follow the strategy proposed previously for the meal kit companies, which delivers better short- and longer-term results, and communicate it clearly and transparently with all stakeholders.

A FIVE-STEP PROCESS TO INCREASE LONGER-TERM PROFITS

Many companies have achieved remarkable results by shifting to a longer-term profit optimization strategy.

Historically, Apple was known for high-quality hardware products. While these products were incredibly successful, the company's revenue was heavily reliant on infrequent customer purchases. After a customer bought a device, the revenue stream from that customer stopped until the next upgrade cycle. As the penetration of the iPhone increased, Apple's phone shipments plateaued as phones became more expensive, competition increased, and customers kept their phones longer.[9]

Recognizing this limitation, Apple shifted its strategy from a hardware-centric model to building an interconnected ecosystem of services designed to enhance longer-term profits. The company launched subscription-based offerings like Apple Music, iCloud, Apple TV+, Apple Arcade, Apple Fitness+, and Apple News+. The introduction of Apple One, a bundled subscription combining multiple services at a discounted price, further locked customers into the Apple ecosystem, encouraging them to use multiple services.

Since the margin for services was around 70 percent, compared to 35 percent for hardware,[10] Apple smartly lowered prices for some of its top-of-the-line phones to encourage more users to use the latest, most powerful hardware because it knew that customers with the latest hardware spend a lot more on high-margin services. An analysis suggests that customers with the latest phones spent approximately $2,400 over thirty months.[11] Since a top-of-the-line iPhone cost around $1,000 at that time, that meant that these customers generated approximately $350 of profit from the phone and $980 from services, for a total of $1,330.[12] As a comparison, a customer who bought an average-priced iPhone and did not subscribe to any services generated approximately $245 of profit over the same time frame.[13] Apple's switch to long-term profit optimization therefore increased the thirty-month profit of a customer 5.4 times.

The following is a five-step process to help your company transition from short-term to longer-term profit optimization without negatively impacting short-term results. As in chapter 1, we begin with the marketing team and discuss other departments later.

STEP 1—CHANGE KPI TO CUSTOMER LIFETIME VALUE

If you could invest only in one project in figure 2.1, which one would it be? Project A that generates $2 million of discounted cash flow every year for five years or project B that generates $1 million of discounted cash flow for the first four years and $25 million in the fifth year?

FIGURE 2.1 PROJECTS ARE
EVALUATED ON LONG-TERM CASH FLOW

	Year 1	Year 2	Year 3	Year 4	Year 5	Total
A	$2M	$2M	$2M	$2M	$2M	$10M
B	$1M	$1M	$1M	$1M	$25M	$29M

Most executives would, correctly, choose Project B because it generates almost three times more discounted cash flow over five years. While most companies analyze individual projects using multiyear cash flow analysis, very few actually use it as a primary company-wide KPI.

Let's revisit our charity example from chapter 1. Charity A, as we discussed, raises significantly more money than Charity B by using a better KPI: net donations instead of ROAS. Now, let's consider Charity C, which adopts an even better KPI: predicted net donations over the next five years.

With this forward-looking KPI, Charity C can implement a much better donor acquisition strategy than Charity A. Charity A, focused on short-term optimization, would prefer acquiring a new donor who donates $1,000 today but never donates again. Charity C, focused on longer-term optimization, would prefer a new donor who donates just

$100 today but is predicted to donate the same amount monthly for five years.

In order for Charity A to start thinking like Charity C, it needs to change its KPI from net donations, the donations raised today minus the advertising investment, to net customer lifetime value (CLV) donations, the predicted future donations minus the advertising investment. In this book, CLV will always refer to a customer's predicted *future profit*. If I mean something else, such as predicted CLV based on revenues or historic CLV, I will specify it explicitly.

Let's examine how a B2B SaaS (software as a service) company would make this change. In that industry, many marketing teams focus almost exclusively on short-term metrics like the number of leads and the cost per lead, like in the dashboard in figure 2.2. On the surface, this company seems to be thriving: It's generating a lot more leads each day, and the cost per lead is dropping significantly. Can you spot the flaw in this approach?

FIGURE 2.2 TYPICAL LEAD-GENERATION
DASHBOARD FOR A BUSINESS SOFTWARE COMPANY

	# Leads	Cost per Lead
Jan 1	250	$95
Jan 2	300	$90
Jan 3	350	$85

The problem is that these two metrics are completely irrelevant. What if the leads are of poor quality and few turn into paying customers? What if the leads do convert to paying customers, but they are for small, unprofitable customers? What if the leads thankfully convert to large profitable customers, but many are outside the ideal customer profile (ICP) and churn quickly?

This dashboard guarantees that the marketing team will focus on the wrong things, more cheap leads. It will also create many problems for the rest of the organization, including:

- **Higher costs:** As the number of leads increases and the quality of these leads likely decreases, the company will need to hire a lot of business development representatives to reach out to increasingly poor quality leads, adding to the cost of sales. At the same time, the customer success team, working with many customers outside the ICP, will need to address a growing set of niche issues, increasing support costs.

- **Mistrust:** The sales team and the marketing team will inevitably start pointing fingers at each other, with marketing complaining that sales doesn't know how to close deals and sales complaining that the leads are of poor quality. And senior management won't be able to tell who's right.

- **Difficulty scaling:** As the company acquires more customers outside its ICP, it will find it harder to scale. These non-ICP customers won't get as much value from the product and will churn at a higher rate. To try to fix this issue, the company will divert precious engineering resources to build features for these non-ICP customers, alienating ICP customers. And by catering to a more complex and often conflicting set of customer needs, the company will lose focus and struggle to develop standardized processes to support efficient growth.

To fix these problems, the company should shift to a longer-term KPI that will take the quality of the leads into consideration. The most popular long-term metric in the B2B SaaS business is the CLV to CAC (customer acquisition cost) ratio. Let's examine that metric. Which of these two companies is doing better? Company A with a 100:1 CLV to CAC ratio or Company B with a 10:1 ratio?

It's another trick question because there's not enough information to figure this out. What if Company A invests a total of $1 million in advertising to acquire customers with a combined CLV of $100 million and Company B invests $100 million to acquire customers with a CLV of $1 billion? Company A generated a net CLV (CLV minus the advertising investment) of $99 million while Company B generated $900 million. Just like ROAS, CLV to CAC (or CAC to CLV) is irrelevant. What matters is the net CLV (CLV minus advertising investment).

Only a very small percentage of B2B SaaS companies use net CLV. A good net CLV dashboard is shown in figure 2.3. This simple but effective dashboard tracks the profitability of a B2B SaaS company's advertising investment by forecasting the five-year CLV of each lead generated by the investment and subtracting the advertising investment. It's similar to the charity dashboard in figure 1.2 but with a longer-term focus. And like the dashboard in figure 1.2, this dashboard compares this year's results to last year's to help maximize the year-on-year improvement.

FIGURE 2.3 BEST-IN-CLASS B2B SAAS
ADVERTISING DASHBOARD
FIVE-YEAR NET CLV

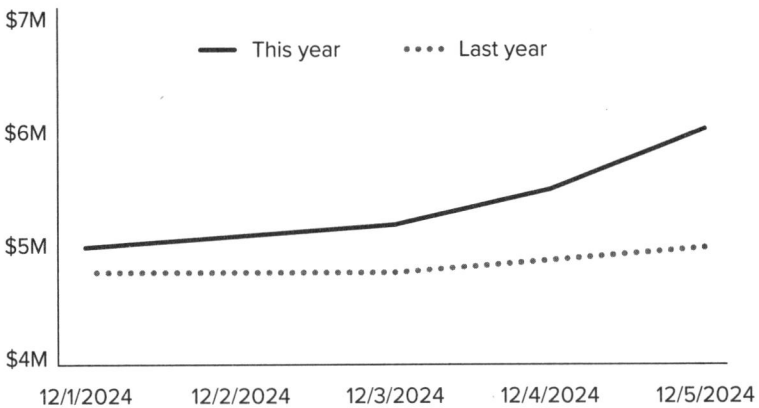

To create this dashboard, a B2B SaaS company would need to develop a lead scoring system capable of predicting, fairly accurately, the five-year CLV of each lead, calculated as the probability each lead becomes a paying customer times the five-year CLV of each of these customers.

For example, in figure 2.4, this fictitious company generated 345 leads on December 4, 2024. Lead 1 is 10 percent likely to become a paying customer, lead 2 is 5 percent likely, and lead 3 is 25 percent likely. If lead 1 becomes a customer, that customer will generate $1 million in CLV over the next five years. Lead 2 would also generate $1 million, while lead 3 would generate $2 million. Consequently, the five-year CLV of lead 1 is $100,000, lead 2 is $50,000, and lead 3 is $500,000. We will cover how to create these CLV forecasts in chapter 3.

FIGURE 2.4 A B2B LEAD SCORING SYSTEM
FOR LEADS ACQUIRED DECEMBER 4, 2024

	Likelihood lead becomes customer	Five-year CLV if becomes customer	Five-year CLV of lead
Lead 1	10%	$1M	$100,000
Lead 2	5%	$1M	$50,000
Lead 3	25%	$2M	$500,000
. . .			
Lead 345	0%	$5M	$0
Total			$6,500,000

Using this lead scoring system, this company can now estimate that the total five-year CLV of the 345 leads it generated on December 4, 2024, will be approximately $6.5 million. If the company invested $1 million in advertising to generate these 345 leads, the net CLV for the day is $5.5 million, which is the data point that was plotted in figure 2.3 for that day.

The same type of dashboard can be applied to almost any business, whether it's a B2C transactional business, a B2C subscription business, or a B2B business. The only difference, as we will cover in chapter 3, is the method used to predict CLV.

STEP 2—MAKE THE RIGHT CHOICES ABOUT CLV

If you choose to use net CLV as a core metric, there are many important choices you have to make. Some choices may increase short-term profits at the expense of longer-term gains, while others may do the opposite. Additionally, certain choices carry higher risks than others. Marketing leaders should work closely with their finance team to make important CLV decisions such as the following.

The Definition of CLV

The best definition of CLV, as discussed previously, is the net present value of future profits. But there may be practical challenges, such as insufficient data, that make it difficult to predict this number. Don't let perfection be the enemy of progress, and identify the best available metric that closely approximates long-term profits. For instance, optimizing CLV revenues (the net present value of future revenues), while not as effective as optimizing CLV, is often better than optimizing short-term profits. The important thing is to optimize the best longer-term KPI possible and to improve it over time as better data becomes available.

CLV Window Length

Determining the optimal CLV window length is a critical decision. A shorter window, such as the few weeks we discussed for a meal kit company, may deliver better short-term profits but risks suboptimizing long-term profits, while a longer window, like five years, can result in the opposite. For example, Amazon chose to optimize its business for the very long term, remaining unprofitable for its first ten years. And it took Amazon sixteen years to recover its $3 billion in cumulative losses. But today, it's one of the most valuable companies in the world, demonstrating the potential rewards, and costs, of a long-term approach.[14]

Ultimately, because of the complex trade-offs involved, the length of the CLV window is a C-level decision.

While companies can optimize only one CLV window at a time, Peter Fader and Neil Hoyne, leading experts on CLV, recommend evaluating CLV from both short-term and long-term perspectives to fully understand the trade-offs. Analyzing short-term CLV allows businesses to quickly assess the impact of current strategies and make timely adjustments. At the same time, focusing on long-term CLV helps organizations develop and sustain customer relationships that drive greater value over time.[15]

Figure 2.5, which illustrates both the one-year net CLV and five-year net CLV, shows that the company is improving both. If the company's strategy focuses on maximizing five-year net CLV, this analysis provides confidence that its long-term approach is also driving short-term improvements.

FIGURE 2.5 SHORT-TERM AND LONG-TERM CLV ANALYSIS
ONE-YEAR AND FIVE-YEAR NET CLV

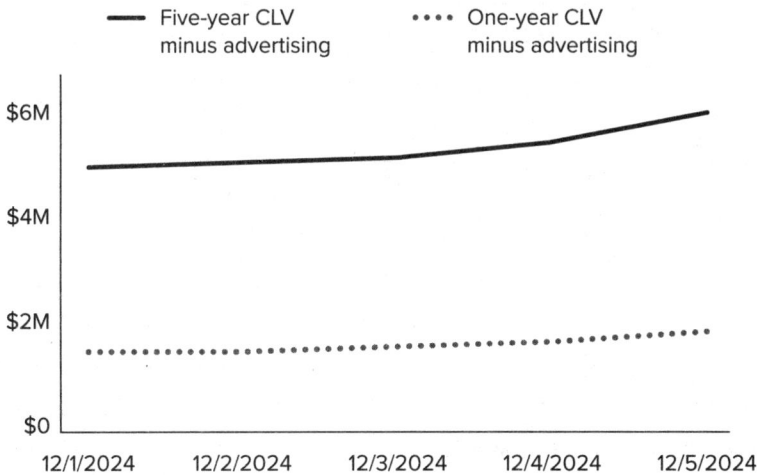

The Level of Tolerance for Imprecision

Forecasting CLV is inherently imprecise. This uncertainty often deters companies from using CLV as a core KPI. To partly address this issue, dashboards should incorporate error bars that clearly convey the imprecision of the data. Management must also establish an acceptable error threshold beyond which the dashboard is no longer trusted.

In figure 2.6, we've improved figure 2.3 by adding error bars, acknowledging the imprecision inherent in the CLV forecast. Over time, as your company's forecasting algorithms improve, the error rate should decrease.

FIGURE 2.6 CLV DASHBOARD WITH ERROR BARS

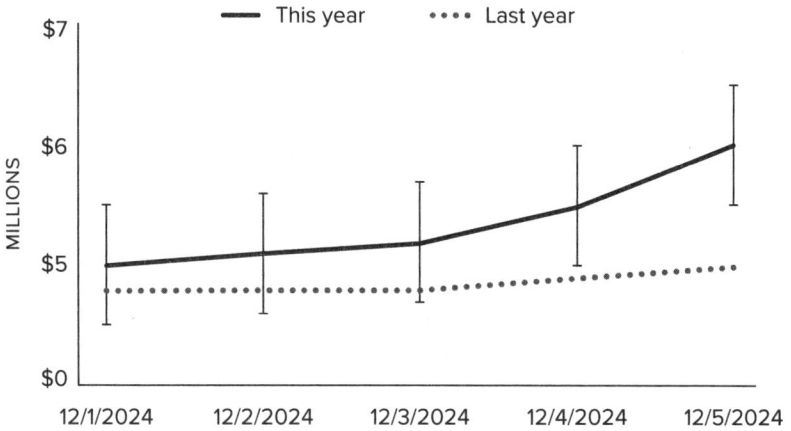

STEP 3—PILOT CAREFULLY, THEN SCALE

Transitioning from short-term profit optimization to CLV optimization can be risky. If not implemented carefully, it may lead to a sizable decline in short-term profits. Therefore, while I advocated for an aggressive pilot approach when shifting from short-term efficiency to short-term profit optimization in chapter 1, I recommend a more cautious and methodical pilot strategy to transition to CLV optimization. Here's how some of the companies I've successfully advised did it.

Start with a Simple Improvement

Before transitioning to full net CLV optimization, start by changing your KPI to a simple, slightly longer-term KPI than the one you're using now. For instance:

- A meal kit company could switch its KPI from "total number of subscribers" to "total number of subscribers not likely to churn in two weeks."
- A B2B software company could shift its KPI from "number of leads" to "number of leads accepted by sales."
- A subscription-based fitness app could change its KPI from "number of new downloads" to "number of new active users after thirty days."

This small adjustment can significantly improve results and is usually easy to understand and implement. It also encourages a focus on quality over quantity and begins the mindset shift from short-term to longer-term thinking. The marketing team should optimize this new KPI for a few months so it can get used to longer-term thinking and demonstrate success.

Do a Simple CLV Test

After that, the first step into true CLV optimization should begin with a simple, low-risk test. A good example would be a test to increase the CLV of 1 percent of the company's current customers who have an average CLV. Since the test involves only 1 percent of the customer base, and these customers are not the company's highest-CLV customers, the risk is minimal.

While the upside is also low, the objective is to get the marketing team to go through the process of optimizing an investment based on net CLV for the first time.

To execute this test, the marketing team will need to learn important new skills, including building a model to forecast the CLV of the test customers, designing a CLV dashboard with error bars to account for data imprecision, and testing multiple ideas to increase the CLV. We will cover how to perform this type of test in chapter 4.

Shift Overall KPI to a Short-Window CLV

After conducting a few successful CLV tests with a small percentage of customers, the marketing team will eventually feel confident shifting its overall KPI to net CLV. A low-risk way to begin this shift is to start with a short CLV window, such as three months.

A charity that is optimizing net donations from new donors could develop a CLV forecast model to predict the donations of each new donor over the next three months. It could then try to maximize the total three-month net CLV of these new donors.

Before implementing this change, it's important that the marketing team collaborate closely with the finance team, because shifting to a longer-term optimization window may temporarily reduce net donations in the very short term.

In figure 2.7, a charity has recently changed its KPI from net donations to three-month net CLV. When it optimized for net donations in the past, it invested $5 in advertising to acquire a new donor giving a onetime donation of $15. This donor therefore generated $10 in net donations. Since the donor didn't donate again, the three-month net CLV was also $10.

After the charity switched to three-month optimization, it invested $20 to acquire a new donor giving $15 each month. While this generates $25 in net donations over three months, two-and-a-half times more than before, in the first month, it generates −$5 of net donations.

FIGURE 2.7 THE POSSIBLE IMPACT
OF LENGTHENING THE CLV WINDOW

	Net donations optimization	Three-month Net CLV optimization
Advertising investment	$5	$20
First donation	$15	$15
Net donations	$10	-$5
Three-month donations	$15	$45
Three-month net donations	$10	$25

Therefore, the switch from net donations to three-month net CLV optimization can radically increase net donations over time but could cause a very temporary decline for a month.

Slowly Lengthen the CLV Window

Once the marketing team demonstrates success with a short CLV optimization window, it can gradually lengthen the CLV window to longer time frames, such as six months, nine months, and beyond. This gradual transition allows the team to validate that CLV is increasing while minimizing the risk of any short-time profit declines. Instead, if a team shifted to five-year net CLV right away, it could dramatically lower short-term profits.

Forecast CLV Conservatively

Another risk in moving to a CLV optimization strategy is overestimating the CLV of customers.

If a charity predicts that a newly acquired donor will contribute $1,000 over three months but the donor ends up giving only $300, the charity will incur a significant loss if it invested $500 in advertising to acquire that donor.

To mitigate this risk, you should forecast CLV conservatively during the early stages of this transition. A simple approach is to reduce all CLV forecasts by a fixed percentage (say, 30 percent) to provide a margin of safety. As the accuracy of the CLV prediction model improves and gains trust, the discount can gradually be reduced and eventually phased out entirely.

Validate the Accuracy of the CLV Prediction Model

It's essential to routinely validate the accuracy of the CLV model. Initially, this might be feasible only at the end of the prediction window (for example, comparing actual donations after three months with the original three-month CLV forecast). Over time, methods can be developed to assess the accuracy of long-term predictions using short-term indicators.

The most advanced companies refine and validate their CLV models at multiple intervals, improving accuracy and building more trust. Google's marketing team used to refresh its CLV calculation every six months. Now, with the help of AI, it refreshes its CLV algorithm two thousand times per day.[16]

STEP 4—USE CLV TO LEARN IMPORTANT INSIGHTS

Some companies use CLV to learn important insights about their business. Here are a few interesting ways to start doing it.

Use CLV as an Early-Detection System

Many companies can't identify significant changes in their business until long after they occur because they analyze only short-term financial or operational data. Some retailers I've advised didn't realize they were losing many high-CLV customers to savvy e-commerce companies until they analyzed CLV data. The financial impact of that high-CLV churn wasn't apparent yet because it fully manifests itself only over a longer period.

By analyzing CLV, companies can detect important changes much sooner because CLV gives them a peek into the future. This is particularly useful in new customer acquisition because it normally takes a long time to understand the behavior of new customers. With CLV, a company can predict the future profitability of new customers from the moment they are acquired, enabling quicker and better decision-making. Figure 2.8 shows the average one-year CLV of newly acquired customers, tracked by their acquisition date. To build this dashboard, forecast the CLV of each new customer acquired (which we will cover in chapter 3) and compute the average each day.

FIGURE 2.8 ONE-YEAR CLV
OF NEW CUSTOMERS ON THE DAY OF ACQUISITION

One-year CLV of new customers by acquisition date

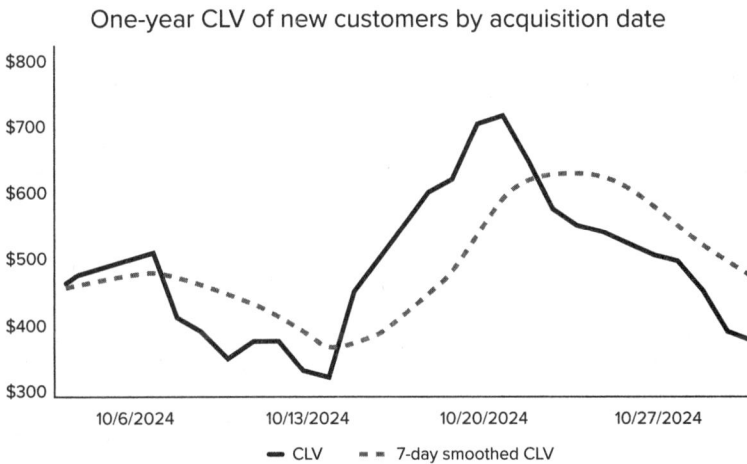

Figure 2.8 shows that the one-year CLV for customers acquired in October 2024 varied significantly during the month, even after the data is smoothed, suggesting that there are important changes happening. At the same time, the daily revenues and profits would likely stay nearly unchanged, masking this fact.

If the company tracks the major initiatives it implemented (for example, adjustments to marketing strategy, promotions, pricing, product offerings, website updates), it can use this information to identify why the one-year CLV of new customers is changing so much. By analyzing figure 2.9, the company could conclude that CLV began to decline when the company made a major change to its website (A), increased again when the change was reversed (B), and decreased again when a new pricing structure was unveiled (C).

FIGURE 2.9. DETECTING PROBLEMS EARLY ON

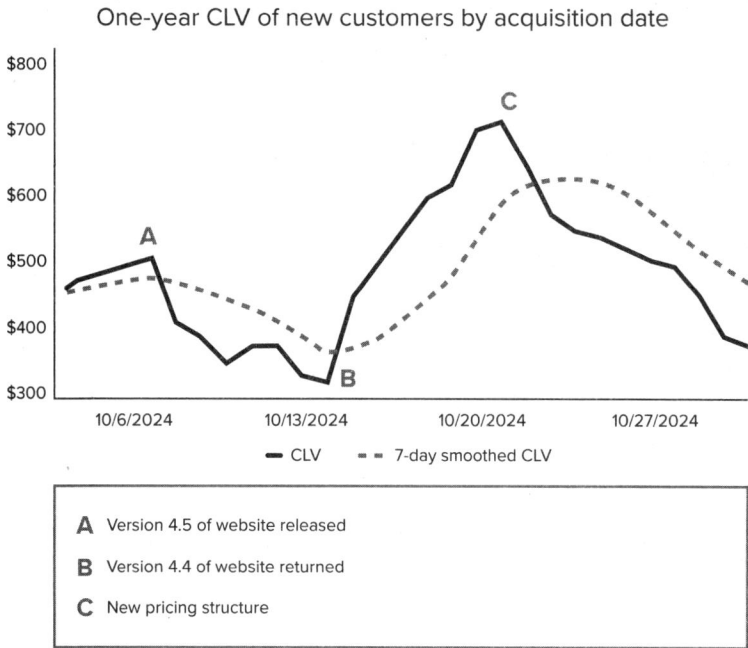

One-year CLV of new customers by acquisition date

A Version 4.5 of website released
B Version 4.4 of website returned
C New pricing structure

Use CLV to Monitor the Health of Existing Customers

Figure 2.10 shows the daily change in one-year CLV of a company's most valuable customers, those in the top quintile of CLV. To build this dashboard, forecast the one-year CLV of all current customers, identify the top 20 percent on the day you want to start the analysis (10/1/2024 in this chart), and calculate the average CLV of these customers every day.

FIGURE 2.10 ANALYSIS OF
THE CHANGE IN CLV OF HIGHEST CLV CUSTOMERS
ONE-YEAR CLV OF EXISTING CUSTOMERS IN THE TOP QUINTILE OF CLV

One-year CLV of existing customers in the top quintile of CLV

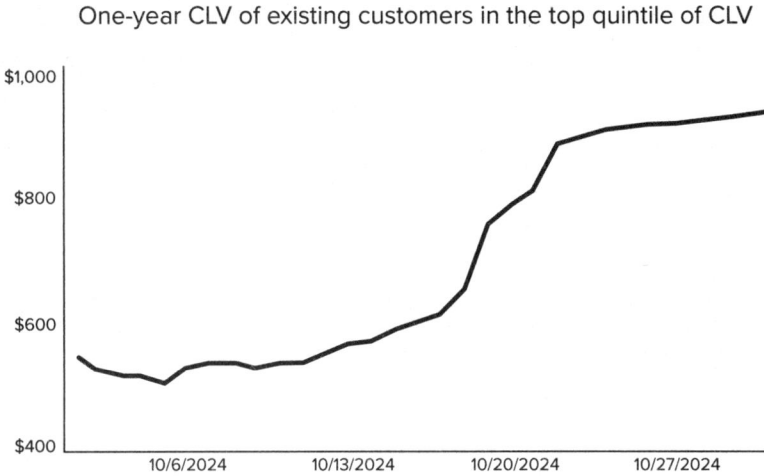

Figure 2.10 shows a significant increase in the CLV of the highest-CLV customers during October 2024, an encouraging trend. Financial statements are unlikely to capture this shift. By tracking key changes in the business, the company could potentially uncover why the CLV of the top 20 percent of customers began rising so rapidly during the week of October 13 and use this insight to replicate the strategy with other customer segments.

The analysis in figure 2.10 can be applied to any customer subgroup, such as those acquired six months ago, customers in urban or rural areas, users of the new version of an app, or customers who experienced negative customer service in the past three months. Some companies have developed systems enabling employees to generate this type of chart on demand for virtually any customer segment. With new generative AI analytical tools like Tableau Pulse, this process has become significantly easier.

Use CLV to Forecast Financials

CLV can predict, often more accurately than typical assumptions-based forecasting, the future profits expected from existing customers. With this information, a finance team can assess how much profit needs to be generated by new customer acquisition to hit financial targets. For example, if the CLV of all current customers for 2026 is $500 million and the financial target is $600 million of profit for 2026, the company needs to generate $100 million of profit from new customers. Using this information, finance can more easily create the rest of its forecasts and budgets.

Use CLV to Value a Company

CLV can also be used to value companies, a concept popularized by Peter Fader and his colleagues.[17] This approach can be used to demonstrate to analysts that a company is undervalued or to evaluate another company during M&A due diligence. The method is relatively simple: Estimate the CLV of the entire existing customer base, a company's total customer equity, and add it to traditional financial metrics, such as assets and liabilities.

STEP 5—EXTEND CLV ACROSS THE ORGANIZATION

Once the marketing team has successfully switched from short-term profit to CLV optimization, it may make sense to spread this approach to other departments. To do it, conduct a CLV Audit and follow the same steps as for the Profit Audit described in chapter 1, but this time shift the KPI to CLV instead of short-term profits. As we suggested for the marketing team, it's important to implement this shift carefully using a low-risk pilot strategy.

Several companies have successfully incorporated CLV into various departments.

Customer Service

Ocado, the UK-based online grocery store, prioritizes customer service interactions by combining CLV and sentiment analysis. Using AI to analyze the tone of customer emails, Ocado identifies how upset a customer is and prioritizes responses to high-CLV, highly distressed customers, ensuring these issues are resolved four times faster than before.[18]

Similarly, American Airlines is rumored to employ a "Helix score," a metric that combines CLV and churn risk, to personalize customer interactions. For example, a frequent flier who stops booking flights, particularly in nonhub cities, signals potential defection to a competitor. Factors like recent flight delays or cancellations increase the Helix score, prompting gate agents to offer personalized solutions, such as compensation, bonus miles, or rule exceptions, to increase the CLV of high-CLV customers.[19]

Some companies even track the change in CLV after every customer service interaction and can calculate the impact of each customer service representative on CLV, an improvement from the "profits saved" idea shared in chapter 1.

Logistics and Fulfillment

Amazon Prime members, who represent a significant portion of Amazon's CLV, get faster and more reliable delivery services. Today, Amazon Prime covers twenty times more products than it did at its launch and delivers twice as fast. Such an initiative would have been impossible if Amazon focused on short-term profits. Instead, Amazon's commitment to CLV has made Prime an essential and hard-to-copy pillar of its extraordinary success.[20]

Product Development

Amazon also uses CLV to improve its products by using their "working backward" process. The process starts by replacing the typical product requirements document with a press release and frequently asked questions, which focuses on customer benefits (for example, customers should be able to check out in less than five seconds) rather than technical specifications (for example, the shopping cart database must be able to handle ten thousand concurrent transactions per second). The product team then works closely with marketing and sales to incorporate customer insights by using surveys, customer service data, and customer panels to ensure new products meet the needs of their customers, with a special emphasis on high-CLV customers.[21]

Human Resources

CLV principles can also guide HR strategies. For example, companies can use CLV data to prioritize training and development programs for employees who manage high-CLV accounts or customer segments. This ensures that the best-trained staff manages the most valuable customers of the future, not the most valuable customers of the past.

BONUS STEP—BUILD OTHER PREDICTIVE MODELS

Once you become confident making decisions based on predictive models like CLV, you should look for opportunities to apply this approach across your entire business. Most companies steer by looking in the rearview mirror (financial statements). Some focus on what's visible through the windshield to understand current conditions (operational metrics). But only a few rely on an AI navigation system that forecasts the road ahead (predictive models). Those that do are going to win the race.

The books *Prediction Machines: The Simple Economics of Artificial Intelligence*[22] and *Predictive Analytics: The Power to Predict Who Will Click, Buy, Lie, or Die*[23] are great references. There are countless predictive models, including long-established ones like churn prediction and next-best-action models. Recent advancements in AI have unlocked a nearly limitless range of new possibilities. Here are a few intriguing examples:

- **Predicting soil fertility:** AI models can analyze satellite imagery, soil samples, and climate data to predict soil fertility and recommend crop rotations, fertilizers, and irrigation schedules. Farmers use these models to maximize yields while reducing resource use and environmental impact.[24]

- **Anticipating fashion trends:** AI can analyze social media, runway images, and consumer sentiment to predict upcoming fashion trends. These AI models allow brands to design products that align with future consumer demand, reducing waste and overproduction. A well-known fashion design house used this tool to design a new skirt collection and increased sales by 9 percent.[25]

- **Predicting the cost of car repairs:** AI can analyze photos of a car accident and, in approximately 70 percent of the cases, accurately assess the repair cost in seconds, without any human involvement.[26]

- **Improving personalized medicine:** AI can predict, with increasing accuracy, the effectiveness of specific treatments for individual patients based on their unique genetic and health profiles. For instance, in cancer treatment, AI can analyze genetic mutations and past treatment outcomes to recommend the most effective therapy.[27]

- **Predicting equipment failure:** In industrial settings, predictive maintenance powered by AI anticipates when machinery or trucks are likely to fail. By analyzing sensor data, operational logs, and historical maintenance records, AI can reduce downtime and maintenance costs.[28]

- Predicting flood patterns: Google has developed an AI-based flood forecasting system that predicts flood patterns. The system combines hydrological data such as rainfall, river levels, and terrain with weather forecasts to model and predict with high accuracy where and when floods might occur. By providing real-time warnings, the system helps at-risk populations take proactive measures to minimize damage and save lives.[29] A similar system could potentially be used by insurance companies to minimize claims.

- Improving the taste of food: IntelligentX, a London-based company, uses AI to improve beer recipes by analyzing customer feedback. Their algorithm processes data from consumer reviews to adjust brewing parameters, resulting in beers that evolve based on drinker preferences.[30] Gastrograph uses AI to model human sensory perceptions of flavor, aroma, and texture, predicting consumer preferences with high accuracy. Gastrograph then gives specific recommendations on how to modify a recipe to align with consumer tastes in a particular region. By reducing the need for traditional tasting panels, Gastrograph enables a more rapid, accurate, and cost-effective approach to product development. I'm not sure if their AI considers consumers' health when making recommendations, but it should.

3

ACQUIRE THE MOST
VALUABLE CUSTOMERS

E ach tree variety has different growth potential. The world's tallest
bonsai is only sixteen feet tall whereas the average sequoia is three
hundred feet high, nearly twenty times taller. For a company to become
a sequoia, it has to behave like a sequoia from the start, at the customer
acquisition stage.

Corporate sequoias understand that a minority of customers in their
industry account for the majority of profits, and they focus on acquiring
as many of these high-CLV customers as possible. Bonsai, on the other
hand, want to acquire as many customers as possible at the lowest customer acquisition cost possible.

Do you know why Jeff Bezos chose books when he launched
Amazon? In 1995, as recounted by Roger Doeren, the owner of a book-
store in Kansas City, Jeff Bezos apparently said that "Amazon intended to
sell books as a way of gathering data on affluent, educated shoppers. . . .
After collecting data on millions of customers, Amazon could figure out
how to sell everything else."[1] This was a simple but powerful insight:

Customers who buy a lot of books are likely to buy a lot of everything. By acquiring these high-CLV customers first, Amazon had a base of customers more likely to spend in other categories as it expanded. Who knows where Amazon would be today if it had selected music as its first category, as music buyers were much less affluent than book buyers back in 1995.

Rick Shadyac expressed a similar sentiment, though with a very different focus: "I realized that the St. Jude mission is so important, it must endure for generations. That's why our fundraising isn't about squeezing every penny from donors; it's about cultivating meaningful, lasting relationships so they remain committed to helping children for the long haul."

INSURTECH COMPANY SUREX
IMPROVES NEW CUSTOMER QUALITY BY 90 PERCENT

For most car insurance companies, a small percentage of customers account for the majority of losses. Acquiring fewer of these high-risk customers can significantly boost profitability. This situation is similar to that of meal kit companies acquiring fewer customers who will churn after the introductory 60 percent off promotion, but it is far more extreme, since a single car accident can cost millions in claims.[2]

Surex, an online insurance broker in Canada, connects consumers with the best policies from multiple insurers.[3] As the insurance market became less profitable in certain parts of Canada, Surex recognized the need to change its strategy from generating as many policies as possible for its insurance company partners to generating as many profitable policies as possible.

As Rob Buchanan, SVP of marketing and demand generation at Surex explains, "Our goal is to build long-term, mutually beneficial relationships with our insurance company partners. That's why we've shifted our focus to the customer lifetime value of the customers we acquire on their behalf, rather than acquiring as many policies as possible."

To achieve this, Surex developed an algorithm to predict the CLV of each new policyholder, assessing factors such as the likelihood of the customer defaulting on their premium payments, churning early, or having a significant car accident. The algorithm uses data like the customer's credit score, their address, the car they drive, and their driving history. While the algorithm is specific to the car insurance industry, later in this chapter we will cover how to build a similar model applicable to your industry.

This algorithm assigns each customer a score from 0 (very low CLV) to 10 (very high CLV). This score is shared, in a privacy-friendly way, with Google, which uses it to train the AI in its ads platform to automatically show fewer ads to customers with a low score and more ads to customers with a high score (we will cover how this works next). The impact of this strategy has been extraordinary. Within a year, Surex acquired 60 percent fewer low-CLV customers (scores of 0–2) and 90 percent more high-CLV customers (scores of 8–10), quadrupling its overall profits. As a next step, Surex plans to work with its insurance company partners to align incentives by getting compensated based on the CLV of the customers they acquire on their behalf.

WHY DO SO FEW COMPANIES
FOCUS ON ACQUIRING HIGH-CLV CUSTOMERS?

If a relatively small company like Surex can achieve such amazing results, why do so few companies focus their customer acquisition strategy on high-CLV customers?

In addition to the reasons outlined in chapter 2 (fear of hurting short-term results, fear of making decisions with imprecise data, and pressure from stakeholders), another reason is that most companies don't know how to do it. While CLV is a widely understood concept, there is surprisingly little guidance on the best tactics to acquire high-CLV customers.

A FIVE-STEP PROCESS
TO ACQUIRE THE MOST VALUABLE CUSTOMERS

Many companies, like Surex, have been able to rapidly increase the CLV of the customers they acquire, including:

- Idom, Japan's largest used car company, increased the profits of their Google investment by 186 percent by acquiring higher-CLV customers. Their strategy was simple yet effective. Since their historical data showed that where a customer lived was the highest driver of CLV, they created a regional marketing strategy with a focus on regions with higher CLV.[4]

- Dish Network increased the profits of their Google investment by 43 percent by using AI to target high-CLV customers who bought online, in-store, or through a call center.[5]

- HomeAway increased revenues by 115 percent in one year by switching their advertising KPI from media KPIs, like conversion rate, to CLV and targeting high-CLV customers with new landing pages and a new advertising strategy. HomeAway didn't share their profit improvement, but it's likely similar to their revenue improvement.[6]

- Indeed, the world's largest job site, increased the number of job posters they acquired by 50 percent. These new job posters were also of higher quality, posting more jobs and paying higher fees.[7]

- Retailer Boyner leveraged Google's High-Value New Customer Mode, a feature designed to automatically target and acquire high-CLV customers, resulting in a 240 percent increase in new customer acquisition and a remarkable 310 percent growth in CLV.[8]

The following is a low-risk and cost-effective five-step process to help your company acquire more high-CLV customers.

STEP 1—UNDERSTAND YOUR INDUSTRY'S PROFIT CONCENTRATION

It's important to understand your industry's profit concentration because it will dictate how much emphasis you should put on acquiring high-CLV customers. In the unlikely scenario that your industry has very low profit concentration (for example, the 20 percent most valuable customers generate only 25 percent of the profits), acquiring high-CLV customers may not be as important as increasing the CLV of existing customers, which we will cover in chapter 4. If, like in most industries, a small percentage of customers generate a high percentage of the profits of your industry, acquiring them should be a top priority.

It's usually easy to estimate the profit concentration of an industry. For example, a simple Google search suggests that 0.15 percent of mobile gamers historically generated more than 50 percent of mobile gaming profits.[9] For a large media company, 2 percent of users were generating 50 percent of the site's total page views and therefore advertising profits.[10] For a billion-dollar retailer, 1 percent of customers were driving 67 percent of its annual revenue (we don't have profit data, but it's likely similar).[11]

A simple ChatGPT prompt can help compare profit concentrations across different industries (see figure 3.1).[12]

FIGURE 3.1 PROFIT CONCENTRATION
BY INDUSTRY ACCORDING TO CHATGPT

Industry	% of Total Profit from Top 20% Customers
High Profit Concentration	
Luxury Goods Retail	80%
Banking (Private Wealth Management)	85%
Enterprise Software (SaaS)	78%
Medium Profit Concentration	
Automotive Sales	65%
Telecommunications	60%
Retail E-commerce	58%
Low Profit Concentration	
Utilities	35%
Grocery Retail	30%
Public Transportation	25%

STEP 2—UNDERSTAND YOUR COMPANY'S PROFIT CONCENTRATION

Surprisingly, some executives struggle to grasp the concept of profit concentration. For instance, I've heard some executives of travel companies dismiss the idea of acquiring high-CLV customers, arguing that their customers book trips infrequently.

While it is often true that the average customer travels infrequently, the top 5 percent of customers travel very frequently and often account for more than 50 percent of a travel company's CLV.

To understand your company's historical profit concentration, begin by analyzing your historical revenue concentration. If your company has reliable customer data, this process should be straightforward.

If the data isn't perfect, use the best available information—it's far better to start with rough estimates than to delay. Many companies have lost significant market share and profits by waiting for a perfect "360-degree view of the customer" before trying to acquire high-CLV customers.

Here's how to estimate your company's historical revenue concentration:

- **Use the right time window:** In chapter 2, we covered the importance of choosing the right CLV optimization time window. Make sure you do your revenue concentration analysis for the time frame that matches the CLV optimization window you chose. If you want to optimize a one-year CLV, you should calculate your one-year historical revenue concentration.

- **Extract all the customers acquired:** Then extract the data from all the customers you acquired at the beginning of that time window (for example, a year ago). If you acquired a lot of customers, focus on the customers you acquired in one day. If not, focus on customers you acquired during an entire week, month, or even quarter.

- **Sort customers by total revenue decile:** Add up the total revenues for each customer since the day they were acquired. Then sort the customers by total revenues and arrange them into deciles. The result should look like figure 3.2.

FIGURE 3.2 ONE-YEAR TOTAL
REVENUES FOR CUSTOMERS ACQUIRED 10/1/2023

	Total revenues ($M)	% total revenues
Decile 1	$100	46%
Decile 2	$50	23%
Decile 3	$25	11%
Decile 4	$12	6%
Decile 5	$10	5%
Decile 6	$9	4%
Decile 7	$5	2%
Decile 8	$3	2%
Decile 9	$2	1%
Decile 10	$1	0%
Total	$217	100%

Figure 3.2 shows that the top 20 percent of customers acquired on October 1, 2023, generated 69 percent of the revenues in the following year, and the bottom 20 percent generated only 1 percent.

- **Create a cohort analysis:** While the analysis in figure 3.2 is interesting, it's only for a specific point in time, customers acquired on October 1, 2023. To get a better picture of your revenue concentration, do a cohort analysis that shows how your revenue concentration has changed over time.

Figure 3.3 shows that the average revenues for the year after acquisition for the top 10 percent of customers acquired in September 2023 increased from $1,500 to $2,000 (left axis). It also shows that the top 10 percent of customers acquired made up 50–55 percent of revenues, which stayed relatively constant (right axis).

FIGURE 3.3 SEPTEMBER 2023
COHORT ANALYSIS FOR TOP DECILE CUSTOMERS

Cohort analysis—Top 10% customers, September 2023

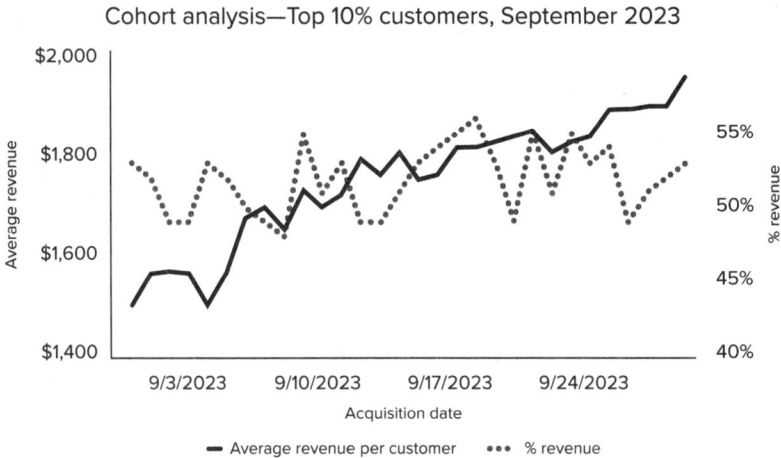

— Average revenue per customer   ••• % revenue

Once you understand your revenue concentration, you can approximate your profit concentration, which can differ significantly. In addition to the story of Steven Rothstein and the AAirpass subscription, there's good evidence that a company's most loyal customers are not always its most profitable. In fact, a high-tech service firm found that more than half its loyal customers were unprofitable. And the correlation between loyalty and profitability has been found to be relatively weak in many industries.[13]

Now that you know the historical revenues of each customer, here's how to turn that into their profitability:

- Estimate the gross margin of each customer: To estimate the gross margin of each customer in a transactional company, subtract the cost of goods of each customer's purchases from the revenues you calculated previously. For nontransactional companies, such as subscription- or contract-based businesses, gross margins are often tied to consumption. For instance, on a streaming platform without advertising revenue, the margin of a customer might decrease slightly as their watch time increases, but the opposite would be true if the platform had advertising. As always, if precise data isn't available, start with a rough estimate and improve over time. For example, a retailer lacking product-level margin data can use average margins by category.

- **Add the cost to serve for each customer:** Understanding the cost to serve each customer can be challenging due to the many variables involved, such as returns, customer service costs, sales costs, and so on. The best way to start is to use estimates and refine the data over time through detailed cost analyses. A hotel chain discovered through a detailed cost analysis that customers accounting for 38 percent of revenue generated 137 percent of profits. Additionally, out of fifty-one different rate types, only three were profitable.[14]

- **Rerun the analysis with profit data:** Once you have the margin and cost to serve data, you can easily re-create the analyses in figures 3.2 and 3.3 using profits instead of revenue. This analysis will yield not just your profit concentration but a list of your most (and least) profitable customers.

STEP 3—FIND THE EASIEST
WAY TO ACQUIRE HIGH-CLV CUSTOMERS

Now that you've identified your most valuable existing customers, how do you find more customers like them? Start by the simplest way to identify high-CLV customers.

Which new customer should a cruise company, trying to maximize five-year net CLV, prefer? A newlywed couple booking a $20,000 ultra-luxury cruise or a recently retired couple booking a $12,000 luxury cruise?

By now you know it's a trick question, right? We don't have enough information to make a decision. But we can venture a guess. Although a cruise company will make more from the newlyweds in the short term, the retired couple is much more likely to take multiple cruises over the next five years.

To use this insight, a cruise company could share a simple customer acquisition rule with Google's advertising AI: They are willing to invest more to acquire new customers over the age of sixty-five. As a result:

- They would likely acquire more customers over the age of sixty-five since they increased their willingness to pay for these customers.

- The average CAC would likely increase as they are paying more to acquire more of these older customers.

- The return on ad spend would likely decrease because these retired couples bought slightly less-expensive cruises than average for their first cruise.

Basically, all the short-term metrics would get worse! And there would be no proof yet that these new, supposedly more valuable older customers would ever buy another cruise. This is where most companies that try a similar strategy get cold feet and back out. It's therefore critical that the executive team focus on the longer-term metrics and ignore the decline in short-term metrics. The payoff is worth it as, in my experience, even a simple change like this can result in at least 20 percent more high-CLV customers.

I worked with many subscription-based companies that had started complex projects to build a sophisticated CLV prediction algorithm for new customers. It was often the case that these companies could already categorize new customers into three groups by looking at their behavior during the first few weeks of their membership:

- heavy users, who typically remain subscribers for years
- light users, who subscribe for months
- quitters, who cancel almost immediately.

Rather than wait for the CLV prediction project to be completed, these companies could simply ask Google's advertising AI system to invest more to acquire heavy users and less to acquire quitters. This simple adjustment can result in a significant increase in the CLV of new customers.

For charities, donors who chose to autodonate every month almost always donate a lot more than others. Charities can therefore significantly increase donations by simply sharing with Google which new donors autodonated and asking Google's advertising AI to invest more to acquire donors who autodonate.

Restaurant chains can analyze customer CLV by zip code. By changing their willingness to pay for new customers by zip code, they can acquire more customers in the higher-value zip codes.

Mortgage companies can share the size of the loan requested by the customer and will acquire significantly more "jumbo loans" customers. Later, they can also share their prediction of the likelihood each application will be accepted, helping them acquire even more "jumbo loans."

For-profit universities can share which prospective students filled out the entire application form and increase their willingness to pay for these leads compared to others who just gave their email. By focusing on CLV, the University of Minnesota's Carlson School of Management increased enrollment 28 percent without increasing its advertising budget. The second year they deployed this strategy, they met their entire enrollment goal for the year by month five.[15]

In many retail sectors, new customers with higher CLV often share specific traits, including the following:

- They purchase items across multiple categories in their first transaction.
- They live in specific zip codes.
- They choose expedited shipping.
- They use gold or platinum credit cards for payment.
- They buy items at full price.
- They select products in the top price quartile of a category. For example, a customer purchasing a very expensive $100 stapler tends to have a higher CLV than someone buying an average-priced $300 desk.
- They buy high-margin, frequently replenished items (for example, razor blades, pet medication, coffee pods).
- They purchase gifts for others. Research indicates gift buyers spend 60 percent or more than average the following year.[16]
- They use the mobile app, resulting in a three-to-five-times higher CLV compared to other customers.[17]

What are the one or two things that are a telltale sign of high-CLV customers in your business? Once you discover that, you can build a simple algorithm to help you acquire more of them. Once you've built this simple algorithm, you can also tweak it based on your judgment or strategic priorities. If your company wants to acquire more younger or older customers, for whatever reason, you can simply add that to your algorithm, which could be as simple as, "We're willing to pay 20 percent more for customers who pay with a gold or platinum card. And if they're also under thirty-five, we're willing to pay 35 percent more." Now share this simple algorithm with all your digital advertising partners and media agencies who will help you translate this business goal into digital marketing tactics, and you will likely acquire a lot more customers like that.

Start-up companies with limited customer data can still try to create this simple algorithm by doing some industry research. Tools like Consensus, which provides access to more than twenty million research papers, can help uncover useful insights. For example, in the restaurant business, consumers who order directly from the restaurant order 35 percent more than customers who order from a third party, customers who order delivery are worth 20 percent more than those who order takeout, and customers who order on an app have a 35 percent higher CLV than those who order on a website.[18] These basic facts should be enough for a new restaurant owner with no first-party data to build a basic CLV model.

STEP 4—BUILD THE BEST CLV PREDICTION MODEL

Starting with a simple algorithm is a great way to generate quick wins. But if your company wants to capture a high percentage of high-CLV customers in your industry, you'll eventually need to develop a more advanced CLV prediction algorithm. This is because advertising platforms like Google, Facebook, Instagram, Amazon, LinkedIn, and others use your data to train their advertising AI. The more accurate your CLV forecasts, the better these platforms can identify and acquire more high-CLV customers for your company. If a competitor has a more precise CLV forecasting model, they are likely to outpace you in acquiring high-value customers.

Here's how it works: You need to share your predicted CLV for each newly acquired customer with major digital advertising platforms in a privacy-friendly way. This data should be provided shortly after acquisition—ideally within weeks, not months—because advertising platforms perform better with timely data. If sharing sensitive profit information is a concern, you can index the data. For instance, leads acquired through LinkedIn ads can be assigned a score from 1 to 100. The platforms don't need to know how these scores are calculated or access the underlying data; they use only the single number you share to assess relative customer quality and refine their AI algorithms to target more high-value customers.

Each advertising platform offers unique tools to help acquire high-CLV customers. In the remainder of this chapter, I will focus on Google, though similar strategies can be applied to other platforms with slight adjustments.

Google has a tool called Maximize Conversion Value bidding that uses AI to maximize the sum of the numbers you share with it minus your advertising investment. The system also provides recommendations for your daily advertising budget to maximize results. Importantly, you can share any metric with Google. For example, if you share the five-year CLV of each customer you acquire, *Google will automatically maximize your five-year net CLV.*

To successfully implement a high-CLV customer acquisition strategy, collaborate closely with your online advertising partners and media agencies. They can guide you through the nuances of integrating CLV data with ad platforms, ensuring the strategy is executed effectively to deliver optimal results. Additionally, they can keep you informed about the latest tactics and tools introduced by ad platforms, making it easier to target and acquire more high-CLV customers as the platforms evolve.

The obvious question you're now asking yourself: But how is it possible to forecast the CLV of a brand-new customer your company has never seen before? Below is a simple and effective way to do it. This method works in almost all industries for companies of all sizes.

Ensure Good Governance

Before you build a CLV prediction model, it's critical to establish governance principles that should include, at a minimum, data privacy rules, data restriction rules, and legal guidelines. Always consult legal counsel and data-privacy specialists before you use any data in your predictive models.

And if your model uses AI, be extra vigilant because additional legal and ethical considerations may apply. For instance, the EU may penalize companies in breach of the EU AI Act up to 7 percent of their global revenues.[19]

Gather All the Data at the Time of Customer Acquisition

When a new customer is acquired, they leave behind a useful data trail. The most valuable data is what you learn about this customer in the first few weeks after their acquisition because, as discussed earlier, advertising platforms like Google and Facebook perform best when they can understand a customer's CLV soon after their acquisition. But as ad platforms become increasingly sophisticated, this may change, and they may be able to leverage data gathered after the first few weeks. It's important to discuss this capability with ad platform representatives or media agencies.

The data used to build a CLV prediction model should include all legally and ethically obtainable information about a new customer, including demographic attributes (age, gender, income, location, marital status, and so on), behavioral patterns (time spent on the website, categories visited, content viewed, app downloads, survey completions, refund requests, reviews, referrals, customer service interactions, and so on), purchasing details (basket size, purchase frequency, categories purchased, price points, discounts applied, payment and shipping methods, and so on), and more.

For B2B companies, the data could include firmographic details (company size, industry, location, revenue, and so on), the role of the contact within the organization, their interactions with the company's website and content (for example, white papers downloaded, webinars attended, demos requested), and their engagement with the sales team (for example, meetings, emails, proposals).

You can also enrich this customer data with legally and ethically sourced third-party data. There are existing databases today that can infer many things about a customer, including their gender, age, and nationality based on their name, with varying degrees of accuracy.

You can change your customer onboarding process to gather data that improves the accuracy of your CLV predictions. For example, a home improvement retailer could offer special perks, such as credit terms and bulk discounts, to customers who identify themselves as contractors and provide their business revenue. By collecting just these two data points, the retailer could significantly refine its CLV forecasting algorithm and more effectively target and acquire large contractors.

Find the Same Data for the Right Existing Customers

Now that you know what data you have when you acquire new customers, a few weeks after they're acquired you need to compare it with the *same data* from customers that have been around for a while. If you're trying to predict the one-year CLV of new customers you recently acquired, find the exact same data for customers you acquired one year ago. Since these customers have been with the company for a year, you also know their actual historic one-year CLV.

Figure 3.4 provides a simplified example of the data a fictitious charity collected about one hundred donors shortly after their acquisition a year ago. The dataset includes each donor's age, a wealth index (ranging from 1 to 10) legally obtained from a third-party database, and whether they opted into autodonations. Since these donors were acquired a year ago, the charity also has their actual donation history over the past year. Assuming these donations have a 100 percent gross margin and no costs to serve, their historic CLV is equivalent to their total donations during the year.

- Donor 1, for example, is fifty-four years old, in the seventh wealth decile, made a onetime $1,000 donation, and has not donated since. Donor 1's historic CLV is therefore $1,000.

- Donor 2 is thirty-four years old, in the third wealth decile, donated $100, and autodonated for nine months, for a historic CLV of $900.

FIGURE 3.4 DATA FROM DONORS ACQUIRED A YEAR AGO

	Age	Wealth (10 = highest)	First donation	Auto donate? (1 = yes)	Number of donations	Historic CLV
1	54	7	$1,000	0	1	$1,000
2	34	3	$100	1	9	$900
3	66	10	$1,000	1	12	$12,000
4	75	10	$500	0	2	$1,000
. . .						
100	29	8	$500	1	6	$3,000

Figure 3.5 provides an example of data for a fictitious streaming service, showing information about customers' subscription plans, viewing behavior during the first two weeks after acquisition, and their total spend over the subsequent year. For instance:

- Customer 1 selected the $15/month plan and, over two weeks, watched one show in one category for a total of twenty minutes, with no children's content. This customer churned after the first month, resulting in a historic CLV of $15, assuming 100 percent gross margin and no costs to serve.

- Customer 2 opted for the $10/month plan and watched five shows across three categories for three hundred minutes, including two hundred minutes of children's content. This customer remained subscribed for the full year, resulting in a historic CLV of $120, again assuming a 100 percent gross margin and no costs to serve.

FIGURE 3.5 DATA FROM
STREAMING CUSTOMERS ACQUIRED ONE YEAR AGO

		First two weeks watch behavior				
	Plan cost per month	Total minutes	Total child minutes	Number of shows	Number of categories	Historic CLV
1	$15	20	0	1	1	$15
2	$10	300	200	5	3	$120
3	$25	600	300	8	5	$300
4	$15	10	0	2	1	$15
...						
250	$25	1,000	50	5	6	$100

Build a Basic Algorithm to Predict the Historic CLV of Existing Customers

To predict the CLV of a new customer, the next step is to create a model that best explains the historic CLV of existing customers, using only the data available when they were acquired.

I've seen many companies spend months, even years, trying to create the "perfect" model. These overly complex models often lose credibility outside the analytics team and end up unused. To avoid this, start with a simple approach, like a basic multiple regression analysis.

If you work for a sophisticated company that is comfortable building and using sophisticated models, you can skip this step and the next two.

Here's the simplest approach I've used to build a CLV prediction model for new customers: I uploaded a dataset of a hundred donors modeled on figure 3.4 (you can find it at https://bit.ly/3ZZ5ss4 if you want to try it yourself) and prompted ChatGPT o1 using this prompt: "Think step by step. Step 1: Use the data age, wealth index, first donation, and autodonate to build a formula to predict total donations. Step 2: Show me the formula. Step 3: Evaluate and report the accuracy of the formula." ChatGPT gave me the following equation to predict the total donations of these existing customers based on age, wealth index, first donation, and whether or not they autodonated:

Total Donations = −2249.45 + (11.55 × Age) + (82.68 × Wealth Index)
+ (3.63 × First Donation) + (4046.68 × Auto-Donate)

This formula can return some negative values, so I improved it slightly by adding that the minimum predicted value should be the amount of the first donation:

Total Donations = Max (First Donation, −2249.45 + (11.55 × Age)
+ (82.68 × Wealth Index) + (3.63 × First Donation)
+ (4046.68 × Auto-Donate)

ChatGPT also showed me that the R^2 for the formula is 0.685, which signifies that the model explains 68.5 percent of the variance in total donations based on the input variables, a good first attempt.

Forecast the CLV of a New Customer

With this simple formula, it's now easy to predict the one-year CLV of a brand-new customer by using the relevant data for that customer. If the charity acquires a new donor that is sixty-five, in the sixth decile of wealth, donates $500, and selects to autodonate, we can forecast this donor's one-year CLV with this ChatGPT prompt: "Using this data (65,6,500,1) and the formula you just created, forecast total donations." ChatGPT predicts that this new donor will donate a total of $4,860 over the next year, including their original donation. Magic!

Test the Model Even If It's Not Very Accurate

Simple models like this one are often not very accurate, leading many companies to discard them completely. But I recommend using these basic models to test whether they can marginally increase the CLV of new customers. You will build more accurate models over time. What matters most initially is not the accuracy of the model; it's to begin shifting the marketing team's focus toward a mindset of long-term optimization. Just ask your advertising platform account team or media agency if they think the simple model will help acquire more high-CLV customers.

Improve Model Accuracy with the Best AI Tools

While tools like ChatGPT or Excel are great for building a basic CLV model, advanced AI tools can significantly improve accuracy. This book won't delve into the complexities of predictive modeling, as it is a specialized and ever-evolving field. But here are a few guidelines.

- **Start as soon as possible:** AI is likely to continue improving rapidly and significantly. The sooner you start leveraging AI to forecast CLV, the better positioned you'll be to master it as AI improves further and as more companies adopt similar strategies. Getting ahead now increases your chances of staying competitive in the future.

- **Leverage automated tools:** Off-the-shelf platforms like AutoML, an AI algorithm that builds AI algorithms, can help companies without extensive data science resources build, test, and validate highly sophisticated AI predictive models.

- **Invest in custom machine learning models:** For organizations with access to skilled data scientists, tools like TensorFlow or PyTorch allow the development of bespoke AI models that often deliver better accuracy compared to off-the-shelf solutions.

- **Consider crowdsourcing:** Platforms like Kaggle enable businesses to crowdsource AI model development to world-class experts. By hosting a competition and offering a prize, companies can attract top data scientists who can help solve complex predictive challenges.

A great example of an advanced AI model is Google Cloud's collaboration with the insurance company AXA to improve their model for predicting large-loss car accidents, those exceeding $10,000 in insurance costs. Using the same dataset AXA relied on, the Google Cloud team augmented the traditional actuarial model that uses the most sophisticated human math for insurance risk modeling with an AI model. The AI model increased the prediction accuracy dramatically, from less than 40 percent to more than 78 percent.[20]

Using this much more accurate predictive model, a car insurance company could build a world-class CLV prediction model for new customers. The model would predict the following for each new customer:

- **Total repair costs:** Using an improved version of the AXA model, a car insurance company could predict how much it will pay in repair costs in the next few years based on the likelihood the new customer will have a car accident (the AXA model described above) and the car they drive and where they live, which influence repair costs.

- **Total car insurance premiums:** A separate AI model could predict how long a customer will stay with the insurer and forecast the discounted cash flow of the premiums over the life of the policy.

- **Profits from other insurance products:** Another AI model could predict the likelihood the customer buys more insurance products and the average expected profitability of those insurance products.

Keep Improving the Model Over Time

Even if a company has a great model, it needs to keep improving it to adapt to changes in the industry, the company, and customer behavior.

One useful method for keeping predictive models up to date is a technique called "windowing," which involves continuously improving the predictive model with the latest data from customers acquired more recently. If a company's original one-year CLV model was built using historical data from June 2023 to May 2024, the model should be updated at the start of July 2024 with data from July 2023 to June 2024. This process should be repeated regularly to ensure the model reflects current trends.

Windowing has an additional advantage: It helps detect sudden shifts in customer behavior if the data from the new month is very different from that of the previous months. These shifts could be caused by external shocks such as a pandemic, major competitive disruptions like the entry of a new market player, or other unforeseen factors. If significant changes are detected, it may be necessary to build an entirely new model using only the most recent data.

Staying up to date with advancements in AI is crucial because new techniques for forecasting the CLV of new users are likely to emerge. To illustrate this, consider the evolution of sorting algorithms, which are designed to organize elements in a random list into logical order. For years, these algorithms saw only incremental improvements. But a breakthrough came when DeepMind, Google's AI subsidiary, developed an AI-powered sorting algorithm that achieved a staggering 70 percent increase in speed.[21]

STEP 5—SLOWLY ROLL OUT
HIGH-CLV CUSTOMER ACQUISITION

Now that you've developed a model to forecast the CLV of new customers, you can start using it to acquire more high-CLV customers. Here's how to do it with the least amount of risk.

Pilot Slowly and Carefully

As outlined in chapter 2, I recommend that you switch from short-term profit optimization to CLV optimization gradually because of the risks involved in the transition. To do that, start with a short CLV window and lengthen it over time, and start with conservative CLV estimates.

In the case of a charity optimizing a three-month CLV, if a donor who autodonates $500 is predicted to donate $6,000 in the next year, the charity could share $3,000 (not $6,000) as the CLV forecast with Google. If a donor who donates $1,500 and does not autodonate is predicted to donate $2,000, the charity could share $1,500 instead. This conservative approach would do two things: First, since all the numbers shared with Google are lower than the forecast, Google's advertising system will be more conservative in general, lowering the risk of this new approach. Second, since the data shared suggests that the first donor is only twice as valuable as the second donor, rather than three times more like the model actually predicts, Google's ad system will increase the bids for autodonating donors by two times, not three times. This strategy will cause the charity to acquire more high-CLV donors while mitigating risk. Even if the predictive model overestimates the value of high-CLV donors, the charity will likely avoid significantly overpaying for them during the pilot phase.

Throughout this process, it is critical to ensure that the advertising budget remains sufficient to acquire as many high-CLV donors as possible, maximizing the overall impact of the pilot.

The next step is to track the CLV of the customers acquired with this new strategy. Figure 3.6 tracks the percentage of new customers acquired by quintile of CLV. It shows that the proportion of new customers acquired that were in the bottom CLV quintile decreased after the launch of a test while the proportion in the top quintile increased.

To make sure figure 3.6 is an apples-to-apples comparison, it's important to keep the quintile thresholds constant, using the values established at the start of the measurement period. For instance, if a top quintile customer's CLV was defined as $10,000 or higher before the test began, this threshold should remain constant throughout, even if overall CLV increases during the test.

FIGURE 3.6 PERCENTAGE OF NEW CUSTOMERS BY QUINTILE OF CLV

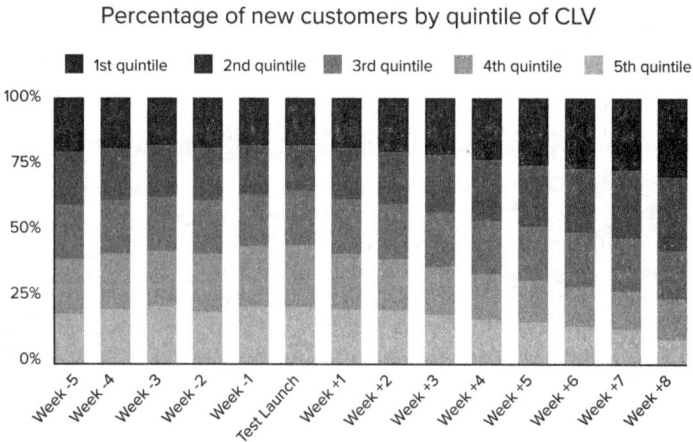

Percentage of new customers by quintile of CLV

In addition to tracking the percentage of high-CLV customers acquired, it's important to ensure that the total net CLV also improves. A great way to do this is by using the dashboard in figure 2.6, adapted specifically for new customers.

Scale Slowly

While the initial gains during this conservative pilot may be small, such as a slight increase in the percentage of new customers in the top CLV quintile and a marginal increase in the overall net CLV of newly acquired customers, results will improve as less conservative data is shared with Google.

Once the charity knows that the pilot has worked, it can start sharing higher CLV numbers ($4,000 for a customer with a $6,000 CLV forecast instead of the $3,000 it's currently sharing). After confirming the continued success of this strategy, it can increase that number to $5,000 and eventually $6,000, the actual forecast.

Lengthen the Optimization Window

Once you're using the actual predicted CLV numbers, you should slowly increase the optimization window. If the charity predicts that a new donor will donate $500 in the next three months and $3,000 in the next three years, it would currently share $500 with Google to optimize its three-month CLV window. Over the course of many weeks or months, it can increase this number by increments, until it shares the three-year CLV of $3,000.

Keep Improving

Even companies that become great at acquiring high-CLV customers will eventually see a decline in the CLV of new customers as the industry's pool of high-CLV customers becomes smaller. The pace of this decline varies significantly by industry; in sectors like retail, it may take years, while in fast-moving markets such as mobile gaming, it can happen in weeks. Here are three ways to reverse this decline:

- Fix immediate problems. As covered in chapter 2, the CLV of new customers can sometimes decline because of actions taken by the company. To address this challenge, you should monitor

CLV trends by acquisition date to detect this problem early (see figure 2.9), identify the root cause of the decline (for example, reduced marketing efficiency, a price change, a change on the website, and so on), and test ways to fix the issue. A great way to see if the root cause is a change in marketing is to look at the CLV across different acquisition channels. If the CLV is declining in only one channel, the odds are that a recent marketing change is at fault. This is usually fairly simple to fix. But if it's happening across all channels, the odds are that there is a deeper issue (for example, a competitor has introduced a better service at a lower price), which can be harder to fix.

- **Test new ideas to increase the CLV of new customers.** Companies should always be testing new ideas to increase the CLV of new customers. For instance, Progressive found that cross-selling other insurance products to current customers significantly increased their CLV.[22] Applying this insight to new customer acquisition, Progressive bundled products right from the start, increasing the CLV of new customers it acquired.

- **Pursue new pools of customers.** Sometimes, there's little that can be done to increase the CLV of new customers. Instead of accepting the inevitable slow decline of their business, sequoias target entirely new pools of high-CLV customers by expanding their offerings. For example, Amazon entered every major retail category, acquiring high-CLV customers who did not buy a lot of books, then it expanded to digital products (for example, movie rentals), and eventually to business solutions (for example, AWS).

BONUS STEP 1—OPTIMIZE PRICING

Another way to increase the CLV of new customers is by optimizing pricing, in a legal and ethical way. But there's a catch: Pricing tests can show that a new pricing scheme increases CLV, but this could be temporary if it's done at the expense of customer satisfaction. This is why, as we will cover in chapter 4, all tests should measure customer satisfaction and CLV. To achieve sustainable CLV growth, consider testing the following pricing optimization strategies.

Test CLV by Discount

A common customer acquisition strategy is to offer discounts on the first purchase or during the initial weeks of a service. While this can increase conversion rates, it may negatively impact CLV. If you have records of different discount rates given to customers you acquired in the past, you can compare the historical CLV across those rates (for example, customers acquired with a 10 percent discount averaged $500 in CLV over three years, whereas those acquired with a 20 percent discount averaged only $300).

If you don't have data on past discount rates, start tracking it and conduct forward-looking tests by creating multiple landing pages with different discount rates and monitoring the CLV of new customers acquired per page. Make sure you run these tests for a long-enough time period since the CLV may change significantly over time as customers who were acquired with heavy discounts have to start paying full price.

I've worked with many companies that changed their discount strategy after discovering that customers acquired through large discounts often have a CLV that is significantly lower.

Test Replacing Discounts with More Advertising

Another clever idea to test is to replace discounts with more advertising. Rather than giving customers a $100 discount on ten thousand jackets that are not selling, a total of $1 million lost in profits, redirect a portion of this amount, say $250,000, to your advertising budget. If this helps you sell all your jackets, you just increased short-term profits by $750,000.

You can also test the impact of this strategy on the CLV of the new customers acquired by creating one landing page with the $100 discount and one without. Then tell Google you're willing to invest 25 percent more to acquire customers that go to the landing page with no discounts. You could then predict the net CLV customers acquired from each page to understand which strategy is better in the long run.

Test the Absolute Price Level

Most companies do price-elasticity testing. But almost all of these tests are done to optimize short-term profits. With the tools we covered in this chapter and the ones we will cover in chapter 4, you can optimize pricing to increase net CLV instead. You could create two different landing pages with two different prices and compare the CLV of newly acquired customers for each page, choosing the price that maximizes the net CLV of new customers. You should also measure the customer satisfaction of the new customers acquired from each landing page to ensure that the page with the higher price does not have noticeably lower customer satisfaction.

Test Pricing Tiers

Offering multiple pricing tiers allows companies to capture different levels of customer willingness-to-pay. Premium tiers with added benefits can cater to higher-CLV customers, while entry-level tiers target more price-sensitive customers. The number of tiers, their features, and their respective price points can be tested and optimized to maximize CLV and increase customer satisfaction.

Test Default Selection and Price Order

Behavioral economics research has demonstrated that default options have a powerful influence on decision-making. Sometimes, making a midtier price the default choice can nudge customers toward a higher-value purchase. Similarly, displaying higher-priced options first and then revealing lower-priced tiers can subtly shift price anchors. This type of price "choice architecture" can significantly increase the CLV of new customers.[23]

In my post-Google consulting work, I worked with an online retailer that tested a redesign of their product pages. The new design included higher priced and higher margin items displayed alongside the item a customer was viewing. For example, page A showed the $90 product the customer was browsing, while page B showed the $90 product and a $150 premium product next to it. Page B led to a 12 percent increase in the sales of the $90 product and sold one $150 product for every five $90 products sold. This single test resulted in a more than 10 percent increase in the CLV of new customers, without any evidence of a decrease in customer satisfaction.

Test New Pricing Models

Many companies are testing innovative pricing strategies, including:

Subscription pricing: Subscription pricing is now being tested in most industries. In e-commerce, the subscription model has evolved from basics like razors to more niche offerings like Introverts Retreat, which curates a monthly box that includes a cozy book, a scented candle, a hot beverage, and bath salts; Mystery Tackle Box that delivers a monthly assortment of lures, hooks, and expert fishing tips; and Hunt a Killer, which immerses aspiring sleuths in a serialized murder mystery, providing clues and challenges to solve a case over several months.

Data from Battery Ventures suggests that e-commerce companies adopting subscription models experienced a threefold increase in CLV compared to traditional e-commerce companies. They also observed that customer retention rates after a year are three times higher for annual subscribers (approximately 50–60 percent) compared to monthly subscribers (15–20 percent).[24]

Of course, subscription commerce can have its downside. It's probably not a good idea to let customers see as many movies as they want for $10 a month if the company has to buy the movie tickets at list price.[25]

Companies are bundling software subscriptions with their hardware. Of course, Peloton has been doing this for years, but the model is expanding to all corners of the house, including the bedroom. Eight Sleep offers the Pod, an intelligent sleep system that keeps each side of a bed at the right temperature for each sleeper. In addition to its $2,300 purchase price, Eight Sleep requires a $199 yearly subscription to access data from its integrated sensors that monitor sleep stages, heart rate, snoring, and breathing patterns, providing users with detailed health insights.

The subscription model has also found success in B2B services. For instance, Adobe Creative Cloud shifted from onetime software purchases to a subscription-based model, allowing businesses to access and update software tools like Photoshop, Illustrator, and Premiere Pro for a monthly fee.

Dynamic pricing: Another innovative pricing model is dynamic pricing, where prices adjust in real time based on factors such as demand, availability, and customer behavior. For example, some ski resorts increase ticket prices on busy weekends to manage overcrowding while offering discounts during quieter periods to encourage attendance. A recent study reveals that this strategy increases a ski resort's revenue by 1.5 percent, which doesn't seem like much but since nearly all of that revenue falls to the bottom line, it can have a meaningful impact on profits.[26] I could not find any study that discusses the impact of dynamic pricing on CLV or net promoter score (NPS), but any test of this strategy should include those metrics.

Usage-based pricing: Another potentially effective strategy is usage-based pricing, where customers pay only for what they use. For instance, cloud service providers such as Google Cloud charge businesses based on storage, processing, and bandwidth usage.

This flexible approach lowers the commitment to get started and encourages continued use as customer needs grow. Publicly traded B2B SaaS companies that primarily charge based on usage have a net retention rate, a fairly good proxy for CLV, of 125 percent versus 114 percent for others.[27]

Usage-based pricing is expanding beyond the tech industry. For example, customers can now rent a car based on the hours or miles they drive rather than a flat daily or weekly rate. Similarly, fitness companies like ClassPass allow members to pay for access to individual classes rather than committing to a full gym membership, and car insurance providers such as Metromile offer pay-per-mile insurance, where customers are charged based on the actual miles they drive.

Customized pricing: Customized pricing is also gaining traction, enabling customers to build à la carte solutions tailored to their preferences. For example, streaming platforms like Spotify allow users to choose from free, individual, or family plans with add-ons for offline downloads or higher audio quality. By offering pricing structures that align with unique customer needs, businesses can enhance customer satisfaction and foster loyalty, leading to higher retention rates and increased CLV.

Mitigate the Impact of Pricing Changes on Existing Customers

Changing your pricing structure can increase the CLV of new customers but may alienate existing customers if not handled thoughtfully. To mitigate potential backlash, companies can adopt strategies such as grandfathering, which allows existing customers to retain their original pricing. In a recent study, researchers demonstrated that subscribers of a video streaming platform informed about their grandfathered pricing remained subscribed approximately twenty-two days longer than those unaware of this benefit.[28]

Alternatively, offering existing customers flexible choices can soften the impact of price increases. For instance, businesses might provide discounted renewal rates, phased-in pricing adjustments, or the option to downgrade to a more affordable plan that still meets the customer's needs. These strategies empower customers by giving them control over their spending while allowing the company to gradually implement higher pricing.

For more information on pricing optimization, read *The Strategy and Tactics of Pricing: A Guide to Growing More Profitably* (sixth edition)[29] and this insightful LinkedIn post by Kakas titled "Dynamic Pricing Strategies Must Balance Profit Objectives with Customer Satisfaction to Ensure Long-Term Success."[30]

BONUS STEP 2—CREATE VIRAL LOOPS

High-CLV customers typically know many other high-CLV customers. Companies that develop simple and effective methods to introduce their products and services to these related customers can significantly increase their acquisition of high-CLV customers.

These "viral loops" are powerful due to their compounding effect. For instance, if a company that acquires a hundred high-CLV customers gets an extra fifteen through a viral loop, it can afford to invest 15 percent more to acquire each of those initial hundred customers. This will lead, in my experience, to acquiring roughly 40 percent more high-CLV customers. Therefore, a company initially projected to acquire one hundred high-CLV customers could instead acquire approximately 161 (100 * 1.15 * 1.40) high-CLV customers thanks to the viral loop.

There are several excellent books on this topic, such as *Hacking Growth*[31] and *Blitzscaling*[32] so I won't go into details, but here are a few good examples:

The best viral loops are natural ones that are part of a product's functionality, instead of being bolted on as an afterthought. Whenever someone uses Calendly to schedule a meeting, the recipient of the invitation interacts with the platform and learns of the platform's benefits, leading to organic user acquisition and faster adoption.

Other viral loops are based on network effects that create more user value as more users join. This is usually very hard to do, so a clever strategy is to focus on microcommunities. A critical factor in Facebook's early success was its focus on getting to critical mass within specific communities. Initially, Facebook targeted students at elite universities (high-CLV customers because they are prime targets for advertisers), which fostered a sense of exclusivity and encouraged rapid adoption in these communities. As Facebook expanded, it built a central growth team, led by Chamath Palihapitiya (now of *All-In* podcast fame), which launched many innovative strategies to accelerate high-CLV user acquisition through viral loops.

One idea was leveraging embeddable badges, which influencers could place on their blogs or websites. These badges displayed a link to the influencer's Facebook profile, which encouraged their followers to sign up to connect with them. This tactic used the power of social proof, as at the time people trusted their favorite influencers more than the relatively unknown Facebook brand.[33]

Another brilliant strategy involved hijacking Google searches. When people searched for friends on Google, that friend's Facebook profile often appeared as the top search result. To view a friend's information, these visitors needed to sign up for Facebook. This tactic allowed high-CLV users to generate new high-CLV users automatically, without even having to invite them to join Facebook.

Another great example was Facebook's photo tagging feature. When someone was tagged in a photo, they received a notification and could view the photo even if they weren't a Facebook user. They were then prompted to create an account to post a comment on the photo, effectively turning a social interaction into a seamless customer-acquisition strategy.

4

IMPROVE THE CUSTOMER LIFETIME VALUE OF EXISTING CUSTOMERS

A sequoia is far more likely than any other tree to grow tall and live a long life. Yet this is not guaranteed. For example, sequoias that fail to intertwine their roots with neighboring sequoias, which helps strengthen their foundation, are at greater risk of falling prematurely.

Corporate sequoias know they won't remain sequoias long if their competitors increase the CLV of their existing customers faster. While the CLV of a customer is in part preordained the day they're acquired, as discussed in chapter 3, there are many ways a company can significantly increase the CLV of some of its customers, especially ones that are already good customers.

FASHION RETAILER INCREASES CLV OF EXISTING CUSTOMERS 45 PERCENT

A merchant at a fashion retailer that had recently implemented a state-of-the-art AI recommendation engine on its website thought of a potential opportunity. She believed, based on her understanding of customer behavior, that encouraging cross-category shopping could increase the CLV of customers who bought from only one category. The AI system, however, because it was designed to maximize conversion rate almost exclusively recommended additional products within the same category the customer was already buying in.

To test the merchant's hypothesis, the retailer identified customers who purchased only in one category and already had an above-average CLV. They divided these customers into a test group and a control group at random and measured the CLV and NPS of each group. The test group had an average CLV of $1,500 and an NPS of 40, while the control group had an average of $1,450 and 41.

The control group received emails promoting additional purchases in the category they had already been buying (for example, more pants/ skirts), while the test group received emails encouraging them to shop in a new category (for example, blouses/shirts).

After a few months, the retailer measured the CLV and NPS of both groups again and the results were clear: The test group's CLV soared to over $2,800, while the control group's dropped slightly to $1,400. Additionally, the test group's NPS rose slightly to 43, while the control group's remained unchanged at 41.

Based on the results of this test, the retailer changed its merchandising strategy to encourage cross-category shopping. For example, they added a "Complete the look" recommendation module that suggested items that complemented the products in the customer's cart, such as a pair of shoes to match a dress. Another module, "Complete past looks," leveraged historical purchase data to recommend products that would complement items previously bought.

To encourage cross-category shopping from the beginning, instead of relying only on cross-selling, they introduced a "Seasonal picks" module, which curated entire outfits perfect for the season, such as sunglasses, sandals, and swimwear for the summer. They also changed their product pages. When a customer searched for "luxury high-heel shoes," they were directed to a page showcasing complete outfits featuring luxury high-heel shoes rather than the typical page with only shoes. The customer could zoom in and even get a 3D image of the shoes so they could examine them closely. But the page was about selling complete looks, not just shoes.

The impact of all these improvements was impressive. Within a year, the average CLV of existing customers had increased by 45 percent.

Increasing the CLV of existing customers also creates a flywheel effect. Once senior management saw that the CLV of existing customers had increased by 45 percent, they asked the customer acquisition team to be more aggressive and increase their willingness to invest more to acquire each new customer. As we discussed before, that led to a large increase in the number of customers, especially high-CLV customers, the company acquired.

WHY DO SO FEW COMPANIES FOCUS ON IMPROVING CLV?

Given these kinds of results, one might assume that all organizations actively try to increase the CLV of existing customers. In fact, 61 percent of companies report that improving the CLV of existing customers is a top priority.[1] But in my experience, very few companies actually prioritize it. Here are some reasons why.

Overemphasis on Customer Acquisition

Many companies prioritize growth metrics like new customer acquisition, often driven by external pressures from investors and analysts. The impact is that marketing and sales budgets are disproportionately allocated to acquiring new customers, leaving little room for retention and CLV improvement strategies. The way to fix this is to budget customer acquisition and existing customer CLV improvement efforts separately and to allocate both budgets based on results, always adding more if an additional investment can increase net CLV.

Short-Term Thinking

The pressure to meet short-term targets leads to a focus on tactics that drive immediate results, such as promotions or discounts. Strategies that improve CLV, such as loyalty programs, often require long-term investment and may not show immediate results, making them less attractive in the short term. The solution is the same as we covered in chapter 3: to change KPIs to longer-term metrics like CLV.

Lack of Data and Insights on Customer Behavior

Companies often lack the tools, infrastructure, or analytical capabilities to understand the buying patterns, preferences, and potential of their existing customers. In fact, a study reveals that only 11 percent of companies strongly agree they can measure the CLV of existing customers.[2]

The result is that many senior executives view their customers as a single, uniform group. In many of my meetings with CEOs, the first question I ask is, "What percentage of your profits comes from your 20 percent most profitable customers?" Only about a quarter of CEOs know the answer. Even fewer can respond to the follow-up question, "What are the three most important things you know about these high-value customers?"

As we will cover in this chapter, companies can get started on a program to increase the CLV of existing customers despite these hurdles by making assumptions, testing simple ideas, and evaluating test results to the best of their ability. Over time, they can invest in a better data and analytics infrastructure.

Organizational Silos

When divisions within a company operate independently, data becomes fragmented, and no one is responsible for the entire customer journey or for maximizing overall CLV.

There are simple strategies to encourage collaboration among different divisions that require minimal coordination but can deliver great results. For instance, an insurance company could mandate that, barring any data privacy concerns, divisions share their customer lists with one another. The home insurance division's customer acquisition team, using the customer list from the auto insurance division, could offer a rebate to those existing customers. This very simple strategy would significantly increase the CLV of these existing customers because insurance customers with two or more products are much less likely to churn, as we will cover later.

While this kind of decentralized CLV optimization is a great first step, it won't maximize CLV. For example, the auto and home insurance divisions are unlikely to create a product bundle together, as this would require substantial changes in their approach. Only a central team, looking at CLV holistically, is likely to create this strategy. We will cover how to create a central growth team in chapter 7.

Lack of Sophistication in Customer Success

Even companies with a centralized team assigned to improve the CLV of existing customers can miss the mark. Most B2B SaaS companies have a customer success team that is supposed to grow existing customers. While some are great at increasing the CLV of existing customers, many focus much of their time on training and onboarding, answering questions, taking customers out for nice dinners, and focusing on contract renewal. While these are all important, they don't leave much time to increase CLV.

To improve the impact of customer success teams on CLV, some B2B SaaS companies are redefining the role to prioritize measurable CLV growth, leveraging predictive analytics to uncover upselling and cross-selling opportunities, and equipping team members with the skills to engage in strategic sales. These companies are also automating as many routine tasks as possible to free up the team's time. Some B2B SaaS companies are also creating dedicated subteams within customer success to drive expansion efforts. And some are even building CLV improvement strategies right into their software, recommending new paid features and upgrades tailored for each customer.

A FIVE-STEP PROCESS TO
INCREASE CLV OF EXISTING CUSTOMERS

Many companies are doing great work increasing the CLV of existing customers. For example, I worked with some retailers that know the impact of hundreds of tactics on their customers' CLV. They know by how much a customer's CLV will increase if they open a credit card, shop across multiple channels, and shop across a new category. They use this data to continuously generate new programs to increase customer CLV.

Progressive insurance has a simple but effective strategy to increase the CLV of existing customers. Their data has shown that the most important action a customer can take, by far, to increase their CLV is to have two or more insurance products. As an example, Progressive knows that auto insurance customers who add a second insurance product stay 1.8 times longer, and 2.4 times longer if they add a third. Progressive calls these multiproduct customers "the Robinsons." The percentage of their customers who are Robinsons has increased by 73 percent between 2017 and 2023, going from 7.1 percent to 12.3 percent. And customers now stay with Progressive an average of nine months longer.[3]

Interestingly, Progressive doesn't sell home insurance—it exclusively offers these policies from unaffiliated third-party companies. Despite this, Progressive is willing to discount its auto insurance, where it generates almost all of its profits, by approximately 7 percent, to convince customers to buy home insurance from another company. Taking this "open insurance" approach even further, Progressive even allows customers to compare competing auto insurance policies directly on its website. This strategy is backed by data showing that customers are more likely to choose Progressive when they can see competing offers. Moreover, even if a customer opts for another insurer, Progressive likely earns a referral fee, which is 100 percent profit.

Allstate learned that 80 percent of its customers didn't know Allstate sold any other insurance products than the one they had purchased themselves.[4] To remedy this situation, they created forty customer segments and cross-sold the right product to each segment. They didn't use complex next-best-action models or sophisticated AI algorithms. They just put customers into segments and sent them different offers.

Using this simple, inexpensive approach, Allstate found that cross-selling was 400 percent more profitable than acquiring a new customer. They then explored other ways to increase CLV, like giving an offer to drivers within a few weeks of their insurance renewal period, which increased retention by 2.4 times.[5]

The retailer Target shared that customers who buy online and in-store are four times more valuable than customers who buy only in store and ten times more valuable than customers who buy only online.[6] Therefore, encouraging customers to shop cross-channel is likely to increase CLV. Many retailers would not understand this fact since their online and store businesses are completely separate.

The following is a low-risk and cost-effective five-step process to increase the CLV of your existing customers. Importantly, it avoids tactics that increase CLV at the expense of customer relationships, like an airline imposing excessive change fees, which can increase CLV in the short term but alienate high-CLV customers who frequently modify their travel plans. Instead, this approach focuses on building sustainable value for both the business and its customers. This is important, as research indicates that companies with the highest NPS in their industry for three or more years achieve revenue growth two and a half times higher (though the study does not provide profit data) and deliver two to five times the shareholder returns over a decade.[7]

STEP 1—FORECAST THE CLV OF EXISTING CUSTOMERS

To increase the CLV of existing customers, it's important to first know what it is today. The good news is that predicting the CLV of existing customers is usually relatively simple, provided you've got access to quality data. While this book won't delve into the details of building such a model, because there are many great resources available on the subject, here's a brief overview.

First, start by forecasting each customer's CLV revenues and then subtract their cost of goods and cost to serve as best you can, as covered in chapter 3. To forecast the CLV revenues of existing customers in transactional businesses (for example, retail, travel, banking), many companies use the RFM model. RFM, which stands for recency, frequency, monetary, predicts future revenues based on the recency of purchases, the number of purchases, and the value of purchases. There are many off-the-shelf RFM models, optimized for different industries. There are also models to help understand the accuracy and variance of CLV predictions for each customer.[8]

For nontransactional businesses (for example, subscription businesses, contract-based businesses), forecasting CLV revenues comes down mostly to forecasting the likelihood of churn. To do that, companies build a predictive model using historical churn data based on customer demographics, customer satisfaction, product usage data, customer feedback, and many other types of data.[9] For example, for B2B SaaS companies, the most important data often includes: feedback from the customer success team, product use that can be tracked down to each click in the product, consumer satisfaction score/NPS, and results from in-product surveys.

The data to forecast the CLV of existing customers is often similar to the data used to build a CLV model for new customers as described in chapter 3. The main difference is that there is a lot more data since many of these existing customers have been around for a long time. I've been a Netflix customer since the day it launched in January 2007. Netflix has a lot of data on my watch history and can probably predict my CLV much more accurately than it can that of a brand-new customer.

AI models can now outperform traditional CLV forecasting models in some industries. Once you've built a simple CLV model using a traditional model like RFM, try to improve results using AI.[10] An AI model was recently able to predict churn in the telecom industry with more than 94 percent accuracy;[11] an AI model predicted the CLV of existing customers for a B2B SaaS company twice as accurately as the previous non-AI model;[12] and an AI model improved the accuracy of CLV forecasting in retail banking by 43 percent.[13]

I recommend you read the article "Expedia Group's Customer Lifetime Value Prediction Model: Understanding Customer Behavior for Profitability" to learn how Expedia built a highly sophisticated AI CLV prediction model that works across all of its brands (Expedia, Hotels.com, Vrbo, Orbitz, Travelocity, Ebookers, Wotif, CheapTickets).[14]

In addition to forecasting the CLV of each existing customer, it's important to update these forecasts regularly to monitor changes in each customer's CLV over time. This information is essential for testing strategies to increase CLV. The CLV model should therefore be inexpensive to run, ideally at least daily, with the necessary resources in place to support this cadence.

STEP 2—SEGMENT CUSTOMERS USING CLV

Many companies segment their customers using demographic and psychographic data in tandem with product ownership data to develop customer archetypes. While this traditional segmentation method is valuable, some companies are now using more advanced CLV-based segmentation methods, including:

- **CLV and customer satisfaction:** Figure 4.1 plots the one-year CLV and NPS of existing customers of this fictitious company. This segmentation can help create specific tactics to increase CLV like calling the highest-CLV customers with the lowest NPS, in the top left corner, so they don't churn.

FIGURE 4.1. SEGMENTATION BASED ON CLV AND NPS

One-year CLV vs NPS

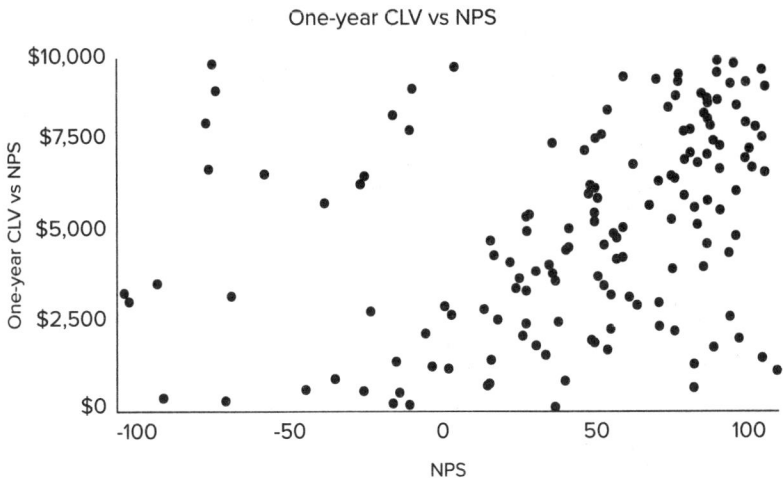

- **CLV and change-in CLV**: Figure 4.2 plots each customer's CLV with their one-month change in CLV. This segmentation can reveal insights that can increase CLV. For example, could this fictitious company replicate the strategies that led to increased CLV for customers in the top-right quadrant (high-CLV customers with a significant increase in CLV in the last month) across other customer segments? Can it avoid repeating the mistakes that caused the decline in CLV for customers in the top-left quadrant (high-CLV customers with a significant decrease in CLV in the last month)?

FIGURE 4.2. SEGMENTATION BASED ON CLV AND CHANGE IN CLV

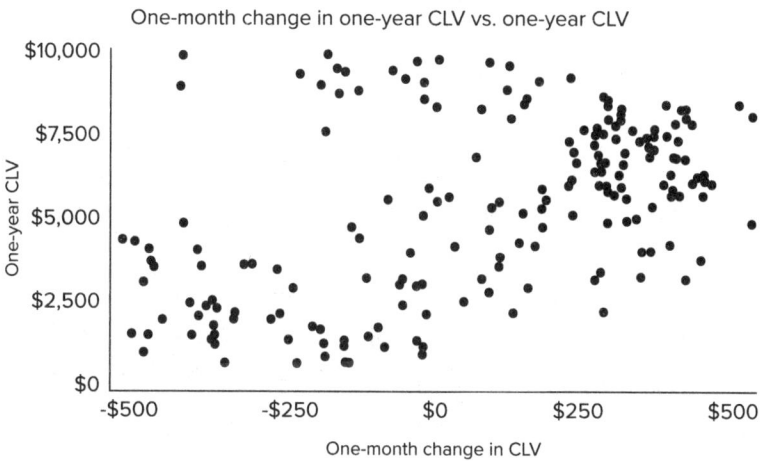

One-month change in one-year CLV vs. one-year CLV

- **Change in CLV and change in customer satisfaction**: Figure 4.3 plots the one-month change in CLV and the one-month change in NPS. This segmentation can reveal anomalies that can shed light on potentially poor business practices.

FIGURE 4.3. SEGMENTATION BASED
ON CHANGE IN NPS VERSUS CHANGE IN CLV

One-month change in one-year CLV vs. One-month change in NPS

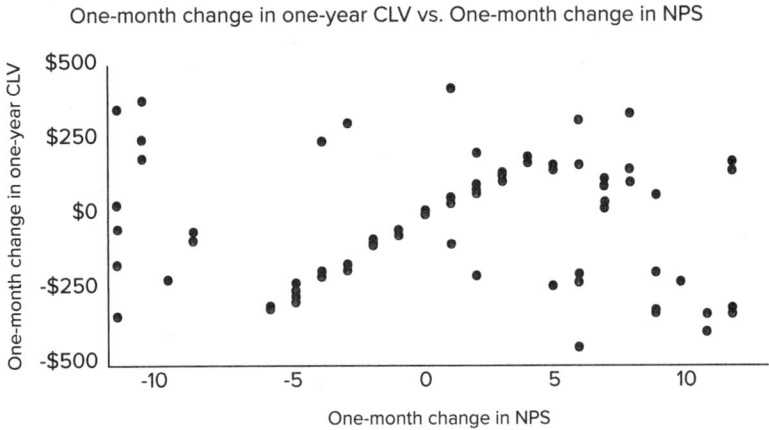

In the top-left quadrant, some customers have experienced a significant increase in CLV despite a sharp decline in their NPS. Is this fictitious company generating profit from these customers at the expense of their satisfaction? What might be driving this disconnect? Conversely, a few customers in the bottom-right quadrant have become notably happier, as reflected in their rising NPS, but their projected CLV for the next year has dropped substantially. Could this be the result of over-generosity, such as offering excessive freebies or discounts, which may be eroding the CLV of these customers?

STEP 3—TEST INCREASING
THE CLV OF HIGH-POTENTIAL CUSTOMERS

Increasing CLV is hard work. That's why it's crucial to prioritize the right customers. While it's possible to increase the CLV of any customer, the segment you should prioritize is your second highest tier of customers roughly in the sixtieth to ninetieth percentile of CLV. There are three main reasons for this:

- **It's easier:** Studies have shown that it's much easier to increase the CLV of high-CLV customers than to try to increase the CLV of below-average customers.[15] This doesn't mean companies should not try to increase the CLV of every customer, especially when using inexpensive tactics like email. It simply means that companies should be strategic and selective in allocating resources for more complex and costly CLV improvement initiatives.

- **It has more impact:** Improving the CLV of high-CLV customers obviously has more impact. If a customer has a CLV of $10,000, a 10 percent improvement is worth $1,000 whereas a 50 percent improvement of a customer with a $1,000 CLV is worth only $500.

- **It's higher margin:** Increasing the CLV of low to average CLV customers is often done through discounting, which leads to low margins and small CLV increases, whereas increasing the CLV of already-high-CLV customers is often done through cross-selling, bundling, loyalty programs, or other higher-margin tactics, which increases CLV even more.

To identify the customers with the most potential, your priority customers, use the data in figure 4.2 to identify the customers who've experienced the largest increase in CLV. Figure 4.2 reveals that the CLV of many customers in the $5,000 to $8,000 CLV range increased over the last month (top right quadrant). Based on this analysis, efforts to grow the CLV should start with this segment, then progress to other segments over time. Of course, while you may choose to focus on priority customers, make sure not to discriminate against other customers as you do.

Once you've identified your priority customers, it's time to generate, test, and scale ideas to increase their CLV. We will cover how to build a world-class testing program in chapter 7. For the purposes of this chapter, I recommend starting with simple ideas that have a high likelihood of success and using the same testing process the fashion retailer used to test category cross-selling.

For example, before emailing an offer to all priority customers, send it to a small, randomly selected subset and measure the change in CLV and customer satisfaction before and after the email for the test and control group. If the test did not decrease customer satisfaction and was profitable, meaning the increase in CLV was higher than the cost of the test, send the promotion to all priority customers. As a bonus, since you've been able to monitor this data at the individual customer level, use it to tailor future offers (for example, send free shipping offers to customer 3455 and complimentary gifts to customer 3456 because that's the best way to increase their CLV and customer satisfaction). You can also identify customers whose promotion costs consistently exceed the resulting increase in CLV and avoid sending them further promotions.

While every company is different, there are a few tried-and-true ways to increase the CLV of existing priority customers that you should consider testing, including:

Pay Special Attention to New Customers

Peter Fader and Sarah Toms, in the excellent *Customer Centricity Playbook*,[16] highlight that risk of churn typically decreases over time. Customers who have been with a company for one month might have an average retention rate of 65 percent, while those with the company for a year could have a 90 percent retention rate. This analysis suggests that retaining new customers, especially ones with a high CLV, should be a high priority.[17]

Predict Churn Better to Lower It

To lower churn, it's important to be able to predict it. Good churn models don't just predict the likelihood a customer will churn but also when and why they are likely to churn.

Using the likelihood-to-churn data, you can segment customers by likelihood to churn (for example, 50–59 percent, 60–69 percent) and test multiple retention offers for each segment. This is often much more effective than sending the same offers to each segment.

Using churn-timing data, you can send offers at the moments that matter the most. Verizon implemented an AI model to predict which customers were at risk of leaving, particularly those facing a rate increase after an introductory period.

Using the reason-for-churn data, companies can address issues before they become problems. To do this, build a predictive model to predict the most likely complaint for each individual order (for example, substandard product quality, delayed shipping). Then use this model to minimize the chance of these issues occurring (for example, using expedited shipping for products with a higher likelihood of late arrival), send the right tailored messages to customers when problems are more likely to arise, and focus on resolving the root causes of churn to achieve a more lasting solution.

Get Customers to Buy in Multiple Categories and Multiple Channels

Diversifying customer engagement across product categories and sales channels can increase CLV. As mentioned, Progressive insurance found that customers with two insurance products stayed 1.8 times longer.

While cross-selling often results in higher CLV, a study showed that one in five customers who buy multiple products or services from a company are unprofitable and contribute to 70 percent of the company's total customers' losses, because they overuse customer service, return products, terminate service contracts early, buy only on discount, or allocate the same spending over multiple products (for example, $10,000 in a savings account that is split $5,000 in checking and $5,000 in savings).[18]

It is crucial not to focus solely on the number of products a customer purchases but to evaluate how their CLV evolves as they buy additional products. Understanding the relationship between product adoption and CLV growth provides deeper insights into which product combinations or sequences drive the highest CLV.

As we will cover in chapter 7, it's important to test this idea with a simple solution before investing in more complex and expensive solutions like the ones that follow.

Implement Next-Best-Action Models

A more sophisticated way to get customers to buy the right products in the right sequence, to increase their CLV and customer satisfaction, is to build a next-best-action (or next-best-offer) model. EasyJet used this approach but made it much more compelling by weaving it into a story. Each personalized email leveraged customer travel data to create tailored messages that recounted individual travel histories, celebrated milestones, and suggested future destinations based on past preferences. For example, "Over the last two years, you spent two weeks in Paris and three weeks in Rome, why not take a trip to London?" The campaign achieved remarkable results, with open rates more than 100 percent higher than standard emails (no information on profits or CLV unfortunately).[19]

Find Your Unprofitable Customers and Don't Advertise to Them

If you can identify your unprofitable customers, you can save a lot of money in paid advertising by not advertising to them. There are more drastic actions you can take with unprofitable customers, including firing them, but firing unprofitable customers is not always the best approach because it can damage reputation, lead to legal complications, or cause you to miss opportunities for long-term profitability. Instead, segment unprofitable customers based on the reasons for their lack of profitability and try to address the root causes. Strategies include repricing, adjusting service levels, or restructuring the value proposition to align with customer needs while getting to profitability.[20]

Redesign Loyalty Programs to Increase Engagement

Loyalty programs that reward frequent engagement rather than just higher spending often increase CLV more. Sephora's Beauty Insider program offers a tiered system where customers earn points for purchases, but they can also earn points through activities like writing reviews, watching beauty tutorials, or attending in-store events. Additionally, the program offers various rewards that increase engagement even more, such as exclusive experiences, birthday gifts, and early access to new products.

Programs that require customers to qualify based on a minimum level of purchase can sometimes increase CLV faster. Net-a-Porter has an EIP (extremely important person) program that caters to its most valuable customers, offering a host of premium benefits. EIP clients enjoy access to a dedicated personal shopper available 24/7, early access to sales, exclusive previews of upcoming products, access to rare or limited-edition items unavailable to regular customers, and invitations to high-profile VIP events. What makes the program particularly noteworthy is its exclusivity—customers must spend at least $10,000 annually to qualify.

AI tools can now create personalized loyalty programs that can adapt to individual preferences, offering tailored rewards or challenges that resonate with specific customer interests and keep them engaged.

Personalize the Customer Experience

A Boston Consulting Group study suggests that retailers using best practices in personalization see up to a four-times sales lift and 40 percent higher average order value (no data on profits or CLV).[21] Nike uses its Nike app to offer personalized workout plans, product recommendations, and exclusive access to limited-edition products, creating a more engaging relationship and increasing repeat purchases. We will cover personalization in chapter 6.

Offer New Pricing Models

As discussed previously, new pricing models like subscription or usage-based pricing, can significantly increase CLV.

Offer Useful Content

Companies that provide useful content to help customers derive more value from their products and services have higher retention, as high as 25 percent more, based on my experience. For example, HubSpot provides a lot of resources to its customers, including in-depth articles on CLV and other marketing topics to help them get the most out of their products and services.

Improve Time to Value

In the B2B space, a seamless onboarding process ensures customers quickly realize value, leading to earlier repeat purchases. For instance, HubSpot uses guided onboarding and account managers to help new clients achieve quick wins with its CRM and marketing tools, followed by upselling additional features or seats as the customer grows.

STEP 4—AUTOMATE IT

Once a successful test demonstrates an increase in CLV, the winning hypothesis should be automated so that it can be consistently and automatically applied to all relevant customers. Once the retailer I introduced at the beginning of this chapter proved that cross-category shopping increased CLV significantly, they should then retrain their AI recommendation engine to suggest more cross-category suggestions automatically.

The best example I've ever seen of CLV improvement automation comes from Google. Google has historically relied on thousands of account managers to help advertising clients improve their results. But as Google's advertising products got more complex, it became increasingly difficult for these account managers to recommend the optimal strategy for each advertiser.

To address this challenge, Google implemented an "optimization score" within the Google Ads dashboard. This score, which ranges from 1 to 100, reflects how well an advertiser's Google Ads campaigns are optimized. Many CMOs now use this score to hold their teams accountable, pushing them to achieve a score of 100.

To help advertisers improve their optimization score, Google uses a sophisticated AI algorithm, to provide bespoke recommendations for each advertiser directly in Google Ads. Advertisers can test and implement each idea with one simple click.

The combination of simplicity and gamification proved to be a game-changing innovation. Advertisers quickly adopted the feature, their results improved significantly, and they invested more with Google. Building on this success, Google introduced an even more advanced feature: allowing advertisers to let Google Ads automatically apply recommendations without needing their approval. Initially, some advertisers were hesitant to give up this level of control. But as the potential benefits became widely known, adoption quickly increased.

This system has been remarkably effective. Since its launch in 2019, Google's advertising revenues have soared from $135 billion to $238 billion in 2023, a 15.2 percent compound annual growth rate (CAGR), compared to a 4.15 percent CAGR for the global advertising industry.

As another example, when Allstate saw customers who bought car and home insurance had a higher CLV, it started aggressively promoting a bundle of car and home insurance for new customers. Why cross-sell when you can automatically bundle from the start? According to Bankrate, this bundle saves customers an average of 25 percent on their premiums, the highest in the industry.[22] Allstate is willing to sacrifice a significant portion of its yearly profits because it understands that customers who buy a bundle are very likely to stay customers much longer and be much more profitable in the long run. Only a company that thinks long term, as discussed in chapter 2, would take this approach.

STEP 5—TEST "CRAZY" IDEAS

While it's important to start with the relatively low-risk ideas described so far, there are other, riskier, even "crazy" ideas that have the potential to dramatically improve CLV and even alter an industry's competitive dynamics.

For example, Amazon customers who have Amazon Prime (two hundred million globally up from one hundred million in 2018)[23] spend 2.9 times more than average,[24] and the ones who use Alexa (Amazon has sold more than five hundred million devices)[25] spend 30 percent more than that.[26] While such a large increase in CLV across so many customers is astonishing, the economics of these programs are far from obvious. First, it's estimated that Amazon has lost $25 billion in its Alexa division.[27] Second, while Amazon made $40.2 billion from Amazon Prime subscriptions in 2023, it spent $17.4 billion to generate streaming content for its Prime members[28] and invested $89.5 billion on fulfillment services in 2023, most of that for free shipping for Prime customers.[29] Assuming that the economics make sense for Amazon, Amazon Prime and Alexa are absolute genius because they:

- **Create customer commitment:** By requiring customers to pay a significant up-front fee, Amazon Prime fosters a sense of commitment. This prepaid fee motivates members to maximize their membership benefits, driving increased engagement with

Amazon's ecosystem. Once subscribed, customers are far less likely to shop elsewhere, creating a lock-in effect that competitors struggle to overcome.

- **Build habitual engagement:** Alexa further integrates Amazon into customers' daily routines, encouraging frequent interactions. Whether it's voice-activated shopping, playing music, or controlling smart home devices, Alexa keeps Amazon at the center of customers' lives, increasing retention by making the ecosystem indispensable.

- **Enhance perceived value through bundling:** Amazon Prime bundles a wide range of services, including Prime Video, Prime Music, and exclusive deals, creating a high perceived value for subscribers. This multiservice offering ensures that customers feel they're getting more than just fast delivery, making it even harder for competitors to lure them away.

- **Are nearly impossible to copy:** Amazon Prime leverages one of Amazon's greatest competitive advantages: its unparalleled logistics network, which delivers speed and cost efficiencies that few, if any, competitors can match. While other major retailers have spent decades perfecting store-focused supply chains, Amazon designed its system specifically for end-to-consumer delivery.

Zappos also did something crazy: It was one of the first e-commerce companies to offer a 365-day free returns policy, including free two-way shipping. In the shoe category, with high return rates (35 percent for Zappos) and expensive shipping, this seems like a terrible idea. But Zappos found that, counterintuitively, its highest-CLV customers have the highest return rate.[30]

Gmail did something so crazy that everyone thought it was an April Fools' joke: free unlimited storage forever.[31] When Gmail launched to the public in 2007, Yahoo Mail had more than 250 million subscribers. Just five years later, Gmail was the number one email provider in the world.

Most industries have their share of "crazy ideas." But companies often avoid pursuing them due to real or perceived risks. However, if you've embraced the long-term CLV mindset outlined in this book, you'll see that bold ideas deserve serious consideration.

If you're willing to explore "crazy ideas," here's a great way to do it.

Crazy Idea Generation

While some "crazy ideas" can emerge organically, it's important to be intentional and create structured opportunities to explore bold, unconventional thinking. One effective approach is to dedicate a full day for a "Bold Ideas Day" similar to the one I attended recently.

I joined the senior management team of a large industrial company at a serene nature resort on the California coast. The day began with a guided meditation session designed to help us open our minds to fresh ideas. An external speaker followed, captivating us with an overview of emerging technologies and showcasing impressive AI demonstrations.

In my session, I focused on a global review of "crazy ideas" being explored in the company's industry and in other sectors.

Instead of having a boring sit-down lunch, we had a chef do a demonstration of futuristic food trends like olives that burst when you chew them, functional beverages infused with adaptogens and mushrooms for stress relief, and 3D-printed chocolates shaped like intricate sculptures, customized on the spot for each person.

In the afternoon, before brainstorming ideas, we delved into valuable customer insights previously gathered by asking high-CLV customers thought-provoking questions like "What would it take for you to entrust us with all your business?" or "If you could wave a magic wand and have us grant you one wish, what would it be?"

To conclude the day, we held a unique and impactful brainstorming session. It began with fifteen minutes of silent individual idea generation, where each participant was challenged to generate as many bold ideas as possible, ideas so astonishing they would captivate the company's most valuable customers and position it to dominate the entire industry. The focus was purely on bold, visionary thinking, without concern for financial viability.

Next, participants voted for their top five ideas in two categories: those most likely to delight customers and those most likely to help the company win its industry. This was done using iPads provided by the facilitator, as all other technology had been banned for the day (with an assistant monitoring emails for emergencies).

Finally, the team reconvened to discuss the top ten ideas that received the highest votes across both criteria, leading to a rich and productive conversation.

While a day like this isn't inexpensive, the company generated three incredible ideas and successfully implemented two of them. The result? Their customers are thrilled, and their competitors are still scrambling to catch up.

To further expand the pipeline of innovative ideas, you can also hold an annual "Bold Ideas" contest, inviting employees at all levels to propose daring and transformative concepts. This not only surfaces new opportunities but also cultivates a culture where bold creativity is celebrated and rewarded.

Prioritize

Crazy ideas should be prioritized based on three criteria:

1. **Potential customer impact:** Will they wow customers and significantly increase their CLV?

2. **Competitive impact:** Do they have the potential to have a large impact and help us win our industry?

3. **Ease of testing:** Can they be tested inexpensively?

There should be no mention of the costs or risks of implementation at this point to encourage expansive thinking. Instead of bonsai thinking ("This idea is too risky"), shift the mindset to sequoia thinking ("This idea could change the game and is pretty easy to test").

Test

When testing crazy ideas, the initial focus should not be on feasibility or economics. The primary question to answer is: Will this idea significantly increase CLV? If the idea doesn't show potential to significantly increase CLV, there's little value in pursuing it further. But if it does, there will be time later to refine the economics and operational details. To test a crazy idea, companies should design the simplest, least expensive test possible to evaluate impact quickly and effectively.

To validate the idea of selling shoes online, Zappos founder Nick Swinmurn took photos of shoes from local stores and posted them on a simple website. When orders came in, he purchased the shoes at full price and shipped them to customers. This test minimized up-front investment while testing the core concept of online footwear sales. It also helped Zappos estimate the level of returns, a key concern in online shoe shopping.

While most crazy ideas are likely to fail, all it takes is one breakthrough to disrupt an industry entirely. Testing these crazy ideas efficiently, using quick, inexpensive prototypes, can lead to innovations that redefine markets.

5

IMPROVE YOUR
BRAND PROFITABLY

S equoias are not just the tallest and oldest trees in the world; they're the most famous. In fact, almost five million people visit national parks every year to see sequoias in California. Sequoias have an amazing brand.

Corporate sequoias are also amazing at improving their brand, which can drive substantial profitable growth. Research shows that leading brands have a 74 percent higher shareholder return,[1] can command a 13 percent price premium,[2] and have an 11 percent higher CLV with each additional point of Brand Health Index, a measure of long-term brand equity.[3]

Unfortunately, improving a company's brand is difficult and often takes years. To do so, companies must offer great products and services, deliver impeccable customer service, develop genuine connections with customers, and embody consistent, positive values.

Exceptional brand advertising can sometimes improve a brand quickly, but the odds of success are low. In fact, a study of 288 TV brand-advertising campaigns showed that more than 80 percent of them were unprofitable.[4]

But I've seen many companies dramatically improve their brand quickly, using a clever advertising strategy. It all started with Invisalign.

INVISALIGN DOUBLES SEARCHES
FOR ITS BRAND IN THREE MONTHS

Early in the pandemic, Invisalign faced a significant challenge. The company relied on dentist offices to sell their braces, but many were now closed. Meanwhile, SmileDirectClub, its top competitor, was not affected because they sold directly to customers. One would have expected SmileDirectClub to gain significant market share, but the opposite happened. Invisalign sales increased 28 percent year-over-year in Q4 2020, beating Wall Street analyst estimates by 43 percent and increasing the market capitalization of the company by more than $7 billion.[5] In contrast, SmileDirectClub's sales fell 6 percent. How did this happen?

Part of the answer is that Invisalign, working closely with its agency Publicis, the Google Zoo team, and Cecelia Wogan-Silva, then Google chief creative evangelist, significantly improved its brand during that time.[6] As Kamal Bhandal, then VP of global brand and consumer at Invisalign, says, "When things took an unpredictable turn in 2020, we essentially had to toss our annual plan out the window. Our strategy needed to switch from driving short-term transactions to building the brand and fostering long-term resiliency."[7]

By testing and optimizing different YouTube branding ads in real time, Invisalign learned which got customers to search for its brand more often, using scientific testing instead of gut feel or customer panels to define its branding strategy.[8] For example, can you guess which of these two ads performed best? One that discusses the scientific merits of

Invisalign (https://bit.ly/4fk9Zur) or one that showcases teens explaining why Invisalign is cool (https://bit.ly/3O3Gr8m)?

The second ad, which speaks directly to teens in their language, performed significantly better. In fact, people who saw that ad were twelve times more likely than before to search for the Invisalign brand.[9] As more people saw the ad, searches for the Invisalign brand doubled nationwide. More importantly, Invisalign searches were now double that of SmileDirectClub (see figure 5.1).

Although this shift in relative brand interest didn't immediately affect sales, it led to a significant market share gain for Invisalign once dental offices reopened.

FIGURE 5.1. INVISALIGN'S BRAND SURGE DURING THE PANDEMIC

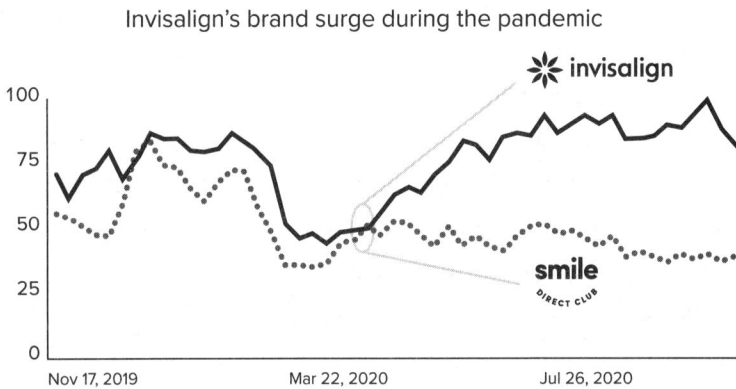

I was astonished by this result. It marked a pivotal shift in how I viewed brand advertising. I often referred to brand advertising as "spray and pray" in the past. Brands would have to commit a significant budget up front, try to reach as many people as possible, and find out only months later if the investment had worked. To me, it seemed more like gambling than a reliable business strategy.[10] In fact, I had never invested in brand advertising as an entrepreneur, a big mistake I now regret.

Invisalign's results changed my perspective. It demonstrated that brand advertising could transform the competitive dynamics of an entire industry when approached with a more scientific, data-driven methodology. The best part: The up-front commitment was minimal, and results could be evaluated and improved in real time.

WHY DO SO FEW COMPANIES DO BRANDING THIS WAY?

Very few brands optimize their brand advertising as scientifically as Invisalign did and still use old best practices from their TV days. As Cecelia Wogan-Silva confirmed, "Fewer than 5 percent of brands I've worked with are leveraging this approach. The other 95 percent still use the tactics they learned in the age of TV brand advertising. The brands using the more modern branding techniques are significantly outperforming the others."

Many brands still think these are the glory days of linear TV, traditional TV broadcasting where shows are aired at a set time. Yet the number of US households with access to linear TV has declined from 100 million in 2014 to 69 million in 2024.[11] I've heard many reasons why many brands haven't yet switched to a highly sophisticated, digital-first brand-advertising strategy, despite the obvious shift in consumer watch behavior. These include . . .

Our Media Mix Model (MMM) Says Linear TV Still Works Well for Us

While MMMs are helpful, they often underestimate the impact of digital advertising. To address this issue, it's important to modernize your MMM to include more granular data, such as data by geography, video platform, ad formats, and audience segments.[12] Hershey's asked its media partners and agency to add more granular data directly to their MMM. This helped Hershey's discover that different YouTube formats performed very differently. By optimizing the mix of YouTube TrueView, Google

Preferred, and bumper ads, Hershey's improved its ROI (no word on profits or CLV) by 40 percent.

It's also important to ensure that your MMM accounts for differences in viewability of different media. And make sure that your MMM accounts for the high ad frequency and significant underdelivery currently generated on linear TV.

Another key consideration is that many MMMs rely on ad impressions to measure advertising impact, but many digital ads are not bought by impression. YouTube TrueView ad impressions are free for advertisers if users skip the ads. To make a fair comparison, the appropriate unit of measurement for MMMs should be paid ad impressions, not ad impressions.

We Can't Drive Mass Reach Without TV

Many traditional TV marketers still believe that TV has greater reach than digital. First, reach isn't the most crucial aspect of a branding strategy. The key questions are: How effectively did you build your brand, and what's the impact on financial metrics?

Second, brands can't drive mass reach with TV. In fact, most struggle to reach even half their target audience. In the auto industry, no auto company was able to get more than 55 percent reach using linear TV, even if they were ready to spend heavily for it. In fact, Toyota invested nearly four times more on linear TV than Subaru but got only four points more reach.[13]

Third, digital has significant reach. Google's marketing team conducted tests to see if YouTube could reach as large an audience as TV by replacing all TV ads by YouTube in a variety of campaigns, regions, and inventory types. YouTube met or exceeded linear TV's reach for more than 85 percent of the five-year age segments.[14]

The only way to achieve mass reach today is through an effective combination of TV and digital. Given the advanced sophistication of digital tools, it's wise to start with digital, conduct extensive testing, and then transfer the most successful ads to TV.

TV Ad Costs Are Lower Than Digital

TV costs (CPMs) may be lower, but are those ads effective? A Kantar study, based on data from 557 brands, suggests an average brand campaign could have been 2.3 times more effective by adding more digital in the media mix.[15] Furthermore, TV CPMs are artificially low because they don't take underdelivery and high frequency into account. In fact, according to Nielsen, the average heavy TV viewers see the same ad twenty-six times.[16]

We Prefer Studio-Produced Content Over User-Generated Content

A study commissioned by YouTube shows that viewers find YouTube's content more entertaining, interesting, creative, engaging, and unique than linear TV.[17] What's even more important is that YouTube can deliver superior results. Data from twenty-three hundred brand-lift studies shows that YouTube drives 3.9 times more searches per ad impression compared to TV,[18] and YouTube Select ads, ads put against YouTube's premium inventory, generated more sales per impression than TV in all US MMM studies conducted by Nielsen.[19]

The tide is reversing as top brands are now making their creative look more like user-generated content. Dior tested two approaches: a traditional ad featuring their brand ambassador Yara Shahidi in luxurious settings, and a more relatable ad where she speaks directly to the camera, mimicking a YouTube influencer. The second, more authentic ad resonated better with audiences and improved brand search lift.[20]

Regardless of whether you agree with these points or not, the core message of this chapter remains: There's a more effective way to approach brand advertising using the latest technologies, regardless of your chosen media mix. Even if your brand-advertising strategy heavily favors TV, the following steps will likely significantly improve your brand.

I've worked with many brands that haven't changed their branding strategy in years, to their detriment. Often, when I suggested to a CMO that they test the new approach to brand advertising we will cover in this chapter, the response was, "That's not how we do it. We take what we did last year, which we think worked pretty well, and we tweak it by 2–3 percent." It's no surprise that the average age of these companies' customers typically increases by one year every year as the average age of a linear TV viewer has increased from fifty-seven in 2015[21] to sixty-five in 2024.[22]

Many CMOs from traditional brands have successfully transitioned to a more digitally focused branding strategy after realizing that their brands were unlikely to thrive again if they did not master digital branding. For some—especially those who had built their careers on television advertising—there was a genuine fear that they would no longer be seen as experts. But I've witnessed many of these CMOs not only adapt, but thrive, as they developed deep expertise in digital as well, often with the guidance and support of their Google account teams.

On the other side of the spectrum, many of the born-on-web brands I've worked with—and all the companies that I started—are so used to focusing on bottom-of-the-funnel performance marketing that they struggle with brand advertising. A former Google colleague captures this problem well: "The performance-driven companies my team works with often lack the patience required for successful brand advertising. They might run a test for a few days, but if it doesn't show a return within a week, they pull the plug." This short-term mindset prevents them from fully realizing the long-term value that brand advertising can deliver.

A FIVE-STEP PROCESS TO IMPROVE YOUR BRAND

Whether you're a brand that's been built on TV and are struggling to shift to a more digital strategy or you're a performance marketer who hasn't been able to make brand advertising work yet, I know that digital branding can work for you.

Many brands have modernized their approach to brand advertising and have achieved similar results as Invisalign.

Quebec City was in a world of hurt during the pandemic as international travel was banned. While domestic travel was permitted, Quebec City struggled to attract Canadian tourists. Consequently, hotel occupancy in the city plummeted to just 5 percent, compared to 21 percent for Montreal and 40 percent for Vancouver.

To try to improve the situation, Destination Québec Cité, the city's tourism board, ran a YouTube branding campaign. They tested multiple ads and optimized them in real time based on results. By July, Quebec City had gone from the lowest occupancy rate in Canada to the highest, 55 percent.[23]

Staying in Canada, Mark's, the clothing store, increased searches for its brand by 43 percent, which eventually increased revenues by 18 percent, following the same playbook.[24]

ABC ran an amazing brand campaign to promote the second season of its show *A Million Little Things*. To attract new viewers, ABC aired the entire first episode of the first season, all forty minutes of it, as an ad, since there's no limit on the length of a YouTube ad. They encouraged viewers new to the show to binge-watch the rest of the first season on Hulu before the new season began. For loyal fans, ABC teased a scene from the first episode of season two to build anticipation. This clever and personalized approach resulted in a 200 percent increase in search interest for the show.[25]

And L'Oréal Canada drove 68 percent more awareness for its brand Olia by testing ads on YouTube Connected TV.[26]

The following is a low-risk and cost-effective five-step process to take your brand to a whole new level. I recommend following these steps initially, but as you gain experience, you can accelerate the process.

STEP 1—SHARPEN YOUR DIGITAL BRANDING STRATEGY

Before investing in brand advertising, it's essential that you have a well-thought-out digital branding strategy to ensure that the advertising investment delivers the maximum impact. This strategy should include at least the following elements.

Focus on High-CLV Customers (Again!)

In traditional TV brand advertising, the best practice is to blanket the airwaves with ads and reach as many people as possible. While this approach might work for products like soap, where nearly everyone needs the same amount and thus has roughly the same CLV, it's not the right approach for many businesses. If 20 percent of the customers in your industry generate 80 percent of its profits, as highlighted in chapter 3, your branding efforts should focus on this high-CLV segment.

Targeting high-CLV customers not only delivers greater impact per customer but is also more cost-effective because branding efforts are concentrated on a smaller, more valuable audience. If customers in the top 20 percent of CLV in your industry are ten times more valuable than average (like in figure 3.2), your company could reach these customers with the same frequency as a blanket all-customer branding strategy for a fraction of your media budget. Assuming you can reach these 20 percent high-CLV customers with only 33 percent of your budget, your branding campaign will therefore be ten times more impactful for only 33 percent of the investment, resulting in a remarkable thirty times improvement in efficacy.

When choosing audience targets for branding, many companies focus solely on demographics, a strategy from the TV days. While a specific demographic (for example, urban women earning more than $250,000 annually) might be a high-CLV audience worth targeting, it's important to consider other nondemographic audience types. A study of YouTube mobile campaigns revealed that ads targeted based on consumers' interests, life events, or in-market status generate 50 percent more brand awareness, 30 percent more consideration, and 40 percent more purchase intent than ads targeted only based on demographics.[27]

Instead of focusing only on beauty enthusiasts, CoverGirl launched a campaign aimed at a diverse range of women based on their interests, like writers, motocross racers, chefs, gamers, and auto enthusiasts, with ads tailored to those interests. This strategy proved twice as effective as traditional targeting.[28] Sonos changed its audience focus from the typical male audiophile demographic to individuals undergoing life events like moving because customers who move are more likely to change their audio system. This strategy led to a 500 percent increase in searches for Sonos.[29] Airbnb targeted consumers in the trip-planning phase, resulting in a 7.5 times increase in brand interest.[30] Minute Maid identified consumers who frequent convenience stores, achieving a threefold sales lift compared to traditional demographic targeting.[31]

Focus on the Brand Metric with the Highest Impact

Once you've identified the high-CLV audiences you want to target, it's important to focus on the right aspect of branding. Should you increase brand awareness, brand consideration, or brand favorability? This is an important choice because the tactics to improve each are very different. While it's certainly possible to try to improve more than one metric, we recommend you start with the most important first and expand from there over time.

To understand what metric to improve first, look for academic studies (or your own internal data) that demonstrate a clear link between a brand metric and a financial metric in your industry. In the car insurance industry, there's historically been a strong correlation, demonstrated in figure 5.2, between the percentage of nonshoppers with unaided brand awareness of an insurance company's brand and the percentage of customers looking for car insurance who request a quote from that company.[32]

FIGURE 5.2 UNAIDED AWARENESS
AND LIKELIHOOD TO QUOTE IN CAR INSURANCE

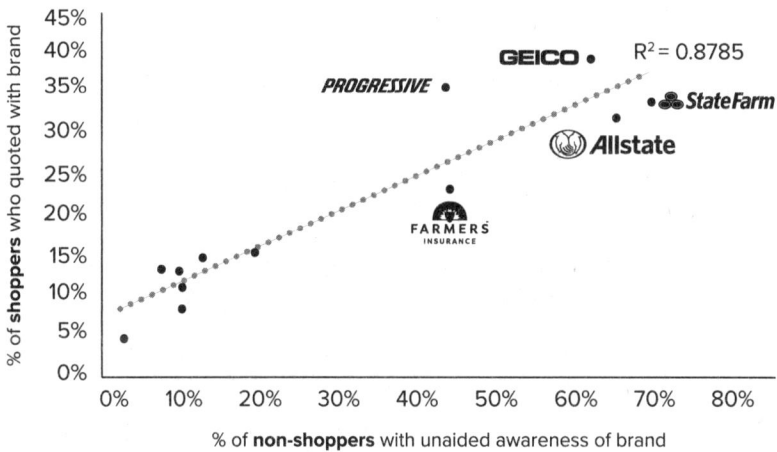

In the movie business, consideration is more important than awareness. In fact, as demonstrated in figure 5.3, the opening box office of a movie increases exponentially as the consideration for the movie grows.[33]

FIGURE 5.3 CONSIDERATION AND OPENING BOX OFFICE IN MOVIES

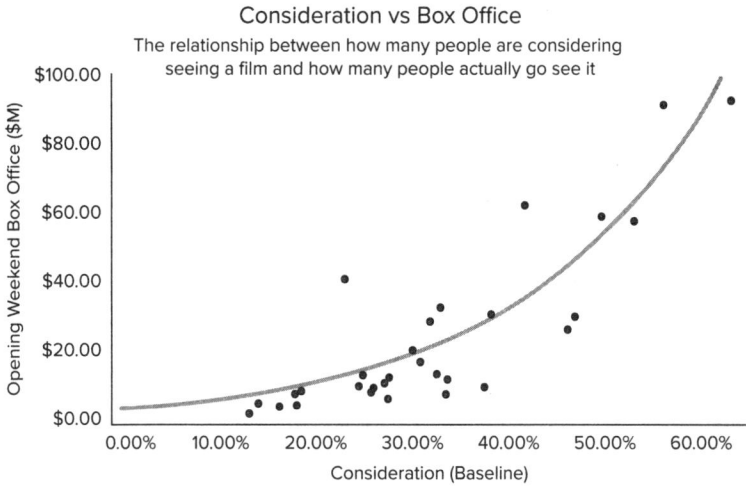

Consideration vs Box Office
The relationship between how many people are considering seeing a film and how many people actually go see it

In addition to identifying the brand metric most closely aligned with financial performance in your industry, it's also important to evaluate your brand's current strengths and weaknesses. For example, while increasing brand awareness might be the most critical metric in your industry, it may not be the best area of focus if your company already has high brand awareness.

For example, figure 5.4, taken from a 2017 study, shows that Bank of America has high awareness (94 percent) and consideration (44 percent) but has relatively low choice (13 percent), the percentage of people who choose to open an account with them. In fact, Bank of America's choice-to-consideration ratio, the percentage of customers who open an account with Bank of America as a percentage of those who consider doing it, is 30 percent, the lowest number on the list. Bank of America should therefore focus on improving its brand favorability metric to increase the percentage of customers who will choose to bank with them. Wells Fargo should do the same. Conversely, Citibank should work on consideration, PNC and U.S. Bank should work on awareness, and Capital One should work on awareness and consideration.[34]

FIGURE 5.4 BRAND METRICS FOR DIFFERENT BANKS

	Aware	Consider	Consider/ Aware	Choice	Choice/ Consider
Bank of America	94	44	47	13	30
Wells Fargo	87	35	40	14	40
Chase	73	32	43	13	40
Citibank	62	18	28	7	41
PNC	34	11	32	9	42
U.S. Bank	32	14	43	5	65
Capital One	31	7	21	3	50

Estimate the Investment Break-Even Point

Once you've identified the audience you want to target and the brand metric you want to improve, it's important to set a measurable brand-improvement goal. One way to do this is by calculating the break-even point, the point where investment in brand advertising pays for itself in the short term. Achieving this breakeven ensures there's minimal financial risk, as any long-term branding benefits essentially become "free" because the advertising pays for itself in the short term.

One way to calculate the short-term break-even point is by estimating the financial impact of a change in a brand metric. For instance, a movie studio can estimate, using the data in figure 5.3, that increasing consideration for a movie from 20 to 30 percent (which Warner Bros. was able to achieve for its movie *Tenet*)[35] would generate an approximate $50 million increase in opening weekend box office revenue. Since the opening weekend is usually half the total box office of a movie during its entire theatrical run, and the studio keeps roughly half of the box office revenues, the additional profit for the studio amounts to $50 million. This means that the value of increasing consideration from 20 to 30 percent, or by a thousand basis points, is approximately $50 million. Consequently, each basis point of increased consideration is worth around $50,000 in the short term. If a brand advertising campaign can increase consideration at a lower cost per basis point, it's therefore likely to be profitable because the studio will then make more money for years as the movie goes into its streaming release.

Another way to find the break-even point is to determine the value of an additional search for a company's brand. For example, if a thousand additional searches for your brand generate a hundred visits to your website, which in turn generate ten purchases and $1,000 in short-term profit, each extra search for your brand is worth $1 in short-term profit. Therefore, if you can generate a search for your brand for less than $1, you're essentially acquiring a new customer and getting all the longer-term benefits of branding for free.

With the availability of cost-effective tools to track brand metrics and brand searches in near real time, you can now optimize your brand advertising investment in much the same way you would your performance marketing. Instead of relying on the traditional TV advertising approach of creating a single ad, precommitting a significant budget, and waiting months to measure results, you can test and improve your brand strategy in real time and commit a significant budget only when there is evidence that the brand strategy is working.

Another approach is by tying together advertising and sales data. Neutrogena worked with Catalina, the consumer packaged goods (CPG) data and marketing company, to combine their Nielsen marketing data with Catalina's proprietary loyalty card purchase data. By optimizing advertising with this real-time data, Neutrogena outperformed CPG benchmarks for awareness and consideration by up to four times and drove a 14 percent sales increase.[36]

As you improve your ability to predict the financial impact of brand advertising in real time, you can loosen the break-even constraint and invest in brand advertising that is unprofitable in the short term but profitable in the longer term. Avinash Kaushik, previously in charge of evaluating the impact of Google's own mutilbillion-dollar advertising investment, says, "Today, we can accurately predict the short- and long-term impact of many of our ad campaigns, either during or shortly after the campaigns. These tools help us make decisions about budgeting, media allocation, and even forecasting demand." Avinash's team achieved this by leveraging AI to analyze years of past advertising data and predict future results.[37]

By the end of this three-part strategic exploration, you should have a set of clearly defined brand objectives for each high-CLV audience. For example, a high-end gym chain could have the objectives in figure 5.5 below:

FIGURE 5.5 BRAND OBJECTIVES

High CLV audience	Brand metric	Starting point	Goal in 3 months	Estimated impact ($M)	Break-even per basis point ($000)
Households who recently moved into $1M+ homes	Awareness	30	40	$15	$150
Women who make $100K+ and love Pilates	Awareness	15	25	$10	$100
People 35–55 who make $150K+ who love tennis	Awareness	25	35	$5	$50

Figure 5.5 shows that this gym wants to increase awareness for its brand from 30 percent to 40 percent in three months for households who recently moved into $1M+ homes. If it can do that, it estimates it will generate $15 million of short-term profit. It's therefore willing to

invest up to $150,000 for every basis point of awareness it gains with that high-CLV audience. The table then breaks down the strategy for other high-CLV audiences.

STEP 2—RADICALLY IMPROVE YOUR CREATIVE STRATEGY

Now that you have a precise set of branding goals, it's time to take your creative strategy to the next level. Getting creative right is critical because approximately 50 percent of the success of a brand advertising strategy depends on the effectiveness of the creative.[38] Without strong creative, the entire strategy will very likely fail. Below is how some top brand advertisers nail their creative strategy.

Rethink Your Brand Positioning

Before optimizing your creative strategy, take the time to reconsider your brand positioning if you can. In 2017, donations to St. Jude began to plateau. Through a detailed and scientific brand scorecard exercise, St. Jude discovered that while its brand was deeply loved, trusted, and respected, evidenced by an impressive NPS of 90, it wasn't well understood. Potential donors didn't fully grasp what made St. Jude truly unique.

The breakthrough insight was that donors needed to understand that, unlike other cancer hospitals, St. Jude provides lifelong care for children and covers all travel, food, and housing costs for their families—entirely free of charge, allowing parents to focus exclusively on their child. Armed with this insight, St. Jude shifted its brand positioning from "saving children's lives" to "so parents can help their children live through the fight for their lives."

This new positioning helped St. Jude return to strong donation growth. The impact has been enduring, as Morning Consult now ranks St. Jude as the most trusted brand in the US. It's also been named the top career choice for Gen Z in the National Society of High School Scholars survey.

Emily Callahan, former CMO of ALSAC, St. Jude's fundraising arm, reflected on this shift: "Frankly, it was the best investment we've ever made."[39]

In 2009, before Emily Callahan was hired, St. Jude was a highly respected nonprofit doing miraculous work. But there wasn't necessarily a reason for someone in France or even San Francisco to donate to this important cause. Then Rick Shadyac hired Emily. "I hired Emily when she was just thirty, and it was the best decision I made. She helped us rethink how we could position ourselves so we could scale and help even more children."

St. Jude successfully repositioned itself from being a single hospital helping eight thousand children annually to a global nonprofit aiming to cure childhood cancer worldwide through its hospital and research efforts. As Rick Shadyac explains, "We opened the aperture much wider and became known globally. Now our donors come from over eighty countries. This transformation wouldn't have been possible without Emily's help in redefining what our brand stands for."

Follow YouTube Best Practices

You're going to test your ads on YouTube before rolling them out to other channels, so it's important that your ads follow YouTube best practices. An analysis of the best eight thousand YouTube ads of 2024, conducted by Google's advanced AI system, Gemini, and prior research on high-performing ads have identified several key factors that increase ad effectiveness.[40] These include:

- **One objective per ad.** Brand advertising ads should focus on increasing only one objective, awareness, consideration, purchase intent, or favorability. In fact, 80 percent of the best brand ads focused only on one branding objective.[41] For brand awareness, focus on a product message, maintain a fast pace, and prioritize entertaining the audience over engaging with it directly. A great example is Flesh's at https://bit.ly/3BFOQMT. For consideration, highlight a single product, give a great product demo, and include a clear call to action, like in this ad for Brita at https://bit.ly/408FR05. To drive purchase intent, lead with a strong product message, get to the point quickly, clearly communicate the product's benefits, and include a direct ask. This ad from Grammarly at https://bit.ly/3PcGpvK is an outstanding example of this approach. For building brand favorability, tell a rich and engaging story using longer formats and connect directly with the audience like Old Spice at https://bit.ly/49SFjyu.

- Follow the ABCD rule:[42]

    A = Attention: Since online ads can be skipped, it's important to start with an impactful, sensory-rich opening to captivate viewers, utilizing elements like bold visuals and sounds to hook them immediately. Cecilia Wogan-Silva says, "You need to punch the viewer in the face right away, hard!"

    B = Branding: Integrate brand visuals early and consistently. Use product shots, logos, and audio cues to ensure the brand is memorable within the ad's context.

    C = Connection: Foster an emotional link with the audience, using storytelling techniques (like humor or surprise) to make the ad resonate on a personal level.

    D = Direction: Provide a clear call to action, guiding viewers on what to do next with direct cues such as graphics or a written message.

Of course, rules are sometimes meant to be broken. An Apple ad that defies several of these rules has gone viral and earned widespread acclaim. The ad, titled "Heartstrings | Apple Holiday | Hearing Aid Feature on AirPods Pro 2," (https://bit.ly/3W5ZEef), runs nearly two minutes, begins at a slow pace (breaking rule A), doesn't show any branding or product until the very end (breaking rule B), and lacks a clear call to action (breaking rule D). Like many exceptional ads, however, its success lies in evoking a deep emotional reaction in viewers (rule C).

- **Celebrate people:** In 2024, many of the top ads focused on celebrating people. The most important best practices included:

    Increase representation: Top ads featured more diverse characters, including people in nontraditional roles and those with disabilities, making brands more inclusive.

    Celebrate self-expression: Top ads showcased individuality and unique styles, often appealing to Gen Z audiences.

    Focus on community: Top ads increasingly depicted themes of deep connection and community, contrasting with pandemic-era isolation.

Test

Google's Media Lab tests all its creative before deploying them.[43] They've standardized their testing, which now includes the use of AI.

- **Predictive models:** The Media Lab uses AI to catalog more than fifty features for Google Ad creatives across various formats (text, audio, image). Features range from basic (for example, brand logo placement) to specific (for example, natural landscapes or abstract language). Using this metadata, predictive AI models were trained with ad performance data, allowing new creatives to be scored on their likelihood to meet a campaign's KPI. The model can predict, with 70 percent accuracy, whether the creative will achieve its goal. This tool reduces the time it takes and the cost to test creative.

- **Recommendations from panels:** When an ad is tested in front of a customer panel, an AI tool summarizes positive and negative feedback into a set of key themes, rates how much people like the creative, and makes creative recommendations for improvement. For example, in a Pixel ad for the UEFA European Championships, the AI flagged that half of the respondents disliked the music. It suggested using alternative music or variations to appeal to a broader audience.

Personalize

Adding simple personalization to YouTube ads can significantly improve brand lift. In fact, for six-second YouTube "bumper ads," personalizing just the text overlay has as much impact as personalizing both text and video.[44] For example, CoverGirl saw that changing the copy of a generic six-second ad for different audiences (for example, women who recently downloaded a dating app, fitness buffs, and women interested in career development) was as effective as changing the copy and creating custom videos for different audiences.

Another simple way to personalize is to change voice-overs for different audiences. Using AI, it's now possible to create hundreds of different voice-overs, in different languages and in different vocal styles, almost for free.

While these simple personalization tricks are likely good enough for your general audience, I recommend you go further with your high-CLV customers. First, break them down into microsegments like we did in figure 5.5. Then change the entire creative (not just the text overlay or voice-over) for each. For example, can you guess which of these two ads for business software vendor Monday.com performed much better for a young audience? This one—https://bit.ly/3DEImOJ—or this one—https://bit.ly/3DFKuWC?

Keep Production Costs Low

As we will cover next, your ads will initially be tested in a very small region. Since they will reach only a limited audience, there's no need for them to be fully polished. Some brands opt to test ads that are just good enough to present to customers. This approach allows them to refine production quality later, once they have a clearer understanding of which ads are most likely to succeed. Sometimes, low production ads are precisely what customers want. B&H created low-budget, real-life ads, explaining how their staff could help customers during COVID. The ads increased B&H's brand awareness by 67 percent.[45]

Another way to keep production costs low is to create ads with interchangeable elements (for example, visuals, voice-overs, or taglines) that allow for quick updates and variations while keeping core branding consistent.

Last, leveraging AI is an essential tool for keeping production costs low. While the use of AI in ad creation is still a topic of debate and may involve navigating legal and copyright issues, you should, at a minimum, use AI to generate ad ideas, draft initial scripts, create storyboards, and personalize voice-overs. As you gain confidence and secure proper legal guidance on copyright and other concerns, you can begin testing AI for full-scale ad creation.

For example, Radisson Hotel Group used Google's AI to generate ads automatically. The result was a 50 percent increase in the advertising team's productivity and a 20 percent increase in revenue in these AI-driven ad campaigns.[46]

Even traditionally conservative IBM leverages Adobe Firefly to produce more than a thousand ad creatives within minutes, a process that once took months. IBM reports a twenty-six times improvement in engagement as a result, which, while not a perfect branding metric, shows the potential of AI.[47]

Build Ads Quickly

There are a number of important reasons why you need to be able to make new ads quickly, including:

- **Test faster:** Even if you follow all the best practices described previously, you're unlikely to be successful at first. This means you're going to need to test and iterate a lot of creative quickly.

- **Make more relevant ads:** Developing new ads quickly will allow you to be aligned with the day's cultural zeitgeist, making ads that are highly relevant. One effective approach is to track trending searches on platforms like Google, YouTube, and X, using these insights to compile a list of creative ideas. Google's Media Lab has built an AI system that identifies spikes in conversations on the internet in real time and automatically generates ideas for campaigns. Marketers can also query the tool to understand specific issues like the sports team or recipes that are trending in a certain region to generate more specific ideas.[48]

- **Keep the momentum going:** After a lot of testing, your strategy will likely eventually work and generate significant lift in brand metrics or searches for your brand. But even the most successful campaigns will lose their effectiveness over time without constant updates. One way to do that is to maintain the overarching brand message that worked best (for example, the Geico gecko) and create numerous fresh variations to keep the creative engaging and relevant.

To move quickly, you need to develop a standardized process to streamline ad ideation, creation, personalization, approval, and launch. This requires seamless coordination among creative teams, media buyers, PR, and legal. The goal should be to create and approve new ads within a few hours, enabling daily launches aligned with the zeitgeist of that moment. Since few companies have mastered this level of speed and agility, it can become a significant competitive advantage.

For brands that struggle to develop this capability in-house, creative ad agencies can be an invaluable resource. Some top brands work with agencies with a proven track record of executing YouTube campaigns that significantly improve brand metrics or searches, the capacity to produce high volumes of ads at a low cost per ad, and show demonstrated expertise in personalization.

STEP 3—TEST IN A SMALL REGION

Now that you've got clear branding goals, understand creative best practices, and have the ability to produce ads quickly, it's time to move into testing. I recommend starting with aggressive testing in a small region. The goal is to try to dominate YouTube in that area because this concentrated approach makes it easier to measure the impact of your efforts while keeping testing costs manageable. Continue testing and iterating in this region until you achieve the brand goal you set earlier.

The following are some best practices that some top brands use to ensure successful testing.

Track Metrics in Real Time

A key difference between this modern branding strategy and traditional branding is the emphasis on real-time tracking and optimization. You should track these two metrics: the traditional brand metric you're trying to increase (for example, awareness) and your brand searches relative to competitors. To track traditional brand metrics, you can use many tools, including brand lift studies, which measure the incremental impact of ads on brand awareness, consideration, or favorability. These studies work by surveying audiences before and after ad exposure and comparing their responses to a control group that hasn't seen the ad. Using YouTube's ad testing tools, you can also evaluate brand lift for specific audience segments, especially your high-CLV audiences.

For tracking brand searches, YouTube automatically reports the impact of individual ads on brand search activity. Beyond evaluating individual ad performance, it's also crucial to assess how your brand searches are doing overall by tracking your brand searches compared to top competitors in the test region, using tools like Google Trends.

Use AI to Maximize Results

YouTube has powerful AI tools to optimize brand advertising campaigns.[49] For example, advertisers that want to improve their brand awareness should use Video Reach Campaigns, which perform 3.7 times better than manually optimized campaigns.[50]

As Gopi Kallayil, Google's chief business strategist for AI, mentions, "Many of the top brands use AI to optimize their brand campaigns. For a while, many didn't trust AI, but now that they've seen the results—significant increases in awareness and/or consideration for the same amount invested—many are all in."

Optimize, Optimize, Optimize

It is unlikely that your initial test will hit the mark, but this should not be a cause for discouragement. Optimizing your creative should be able to significantly increase the efficacy of your results. This can require weeks of hard work, but the payoff is big, so it's important not to give up.

Estimate the Financial Impact

The test has so far focused on improving proxy metrics like brand metrics and searches for your brand, with the hope that improving these metrics would later lead to more sales. But if you've never done this before, you'll have no evidence that this is true. To err on the side of caution, before you make the investment to roll out your strategy to a broader region and other channels, it may make sense to continue testing in the small region for several weeks (or even months) to get a clearer sense of the actual financial impact. The goal isn't a scientific answer but rather clear evidence that financial metrics are improving in the test region compared to other regions.

STEP 4—ROLL OUT AND EXPAND TO OTHER CHANNELS

Once there is enough (but not necessarily perfect) evidence that the test is likely to make financial sense, it's time to roll out the strategy to other regions, other tactics, and other channels. Here's how to do it.

Roll Out the Test Strategy Everywhere

The next step is to roll out everywhere the strategy that has performed best in the test. Many brands do this in one fell swoop (for example, all of Europe), while others scale more slowly, subregion by subregion (for example, Sweden, then Norway . . .). It's important to work closely with the finance team during the rollout to ensure the budget has been pre-approved. The budget should also be flexible based on results.

Some brands, particularly those with significant TV advertising budgets, may question whether a YouTube-only campaign can drive substantial impact. While it's true that a combination of channels is often more effective—a topic discussed later in this chapter—a YouTube-only brand advertising campaign can deliver impressive results. For instance, Nissan Canada launched the Nissan Rogue with a YouTube-only campaign.

They created thirty unique video cuts to convey seven distinct stories, each tailored to specific audience segments. The campaign achieved remarkable outcomes: a 12 percent year-over-year sales growth, a 1.3 percent increase in market share, and an 87 percent lift in search interest.[51]

Extend to Other Digital Platforms

While other digital platforms such as Facebook, Instagram, Hulu, Amazon Prime Video, and TikTok have their own best practices distinct from YouTube's, you can typically adapt your winning YouTube strategy to each platform with minimal effort. This can be done gradually in a test market before scaling across a larger region. As always, results should be evaluated holistically, considering the combined impact of all the channels together, rather than assessing each channel in isolation.

Partner with Influencers

When done correctly, influencer marketing is a great way to improve a company's brand with high-CLV customers. In fact, 85 percent of marketers say that influencer marketing has been effective for them, and only 9 percent of marketers say they will decrease their influencer marketing budget in the future.[52]

Office Depot wanted to increase awareness among parents, students, and teachers. The brand partnered with seven creators, who made videos on varied topics like back-to-school shopping, studying tips, and organizational hacks. While each creator had different concepts, they all focused on increasing searches for the Office Depot brand. As a result, searches for Office Depot increased by forty-eight times among consumers who saw the creator videos. A Google marketing team in Germany launched Google's Pixel 7a phone with a 100 percent creator-led campaign. This was a big risk since it was the team's second largest campaign for the year. As a backup, they had traditional ads ready to go and used them as the control in the testing. The creator-led ads generated a 128 percent higher consideration than the control.[53]

Results are especially good with young consumers, who tend to be skeptical of traditional advertising. In fact, while only 6 percent of millennials believe that online ads are credible,[54] 63 percent say they trust what creators say about a brand more than what the brand itself says.[55]

But since influencers typically get paid up front regardless of results, I recommend you test this tactic carefully with lesser-known (and less expensive) influencers before making larger bets. The good news is that a recent study showed that smaller influencers generated better results (of course, they measured ROAS, not profits or CLV) than larger influencers.[56]

I've also seen a few companies pay influencers based on the results (consideration lift or brand search lift, for example) that they generate.

Heela Gonen, formerly the VP of growth marketing at BetterHelp, the online mental health services company, knew that the company faced the difficult challenge of making online counseling mainstream while building BetterHelp into a trusted household name. A key part of her strategy was to partner with influencers and cultural icons. BetterHelp identified that some of their most valuable potential customers were avid podcast listeners who placed great trust in the podcasters they followed. Recognizing this, BetterHelp began paying podcasters to endorse the brand through nontraditional ads—personalized, "host-read" ad-libs that were loosely scripted around suggested talking points. Undeterred by early challenges, they persisted, knowing that podcasts were a rapidly growing channel with very little advertising competition. They knew that if they could crack the code, it would provide a significant competitive advantage.

After a lot of creative testing and podcast selection optimization, they eventually succeeded. Today, BetterHelp is the world's largest podcast advertiser, sponsoring more than eighteen thousand episodes across more than a thousand different podcasts in 2024.[57] BetterHelp even has its own podcast, *Getting Better: Stories of Mental Health*, which is hosted by therapists Micheline Maalouf and Nadia Addesi.

Another impactful strategy focused on acquiring an important customer segment: Gen Z. This generation has faced significant mental health challenges, as outlined in *The Anxious Generation*.[58] To connect with this audience, BetterHelp partnered with Ariana Grande, who has been open about her own mental health struggles and is a strong advocate for mental health awareness.

Together, they launched an initiative offering one month of free unlimited counseling to Ariana's fans, capped at $1 million worth of sessions. Ariana, participating without compensation, shared the offer with her 350 million followers. The response was overwhelming, and the offer was fully booked within an hour. BetterHelp extended the initiative for thirty-six hours, ultimately providing far more than $1 million worth of free counseling.

The results were remarkable and long-lasting. BetterHelp saw a dramatic increase in brand awareness, performance marketing metrics, and NPS, and they acquired a substantial number of high-CLV customers. Most importantly, BetterHelp made a difference in the lives of many Gen Zs, providing free counseling and access to professional therapy to help improve their mental wellness.

Extend to Linear TV

Once your digital branding strategy has been perfected, it may be time to consider extending it to linear TV. Here are some suggestions on how to do it:

- **Start with remnant inventory:** Before committing to significant investments, some brands test their campaigns using remnant, unsold TV inventory, if possible. This allows for cost-effective experimentation while reaching targeted audiences in less expensive time slots.

- **Target high-CLV demographics:** Linear TV advertising is still mostly purchased based on demographic data rather than the precise audience targeting available in digital channels. To figure out what TV demographics you should target, use data from your YouTube campaigns to see which high-CLV demographics saw the biggest brand lift from your ads.

- **Use the best-performing ad for the target demographic:** By the time you're ready to expand to linear TV, you will have likely tested a lot of ad variations on YouTube. You should therefore have a good sense for which ads resonate best with the demographics you will target on TV.

- **Consider investing in higher production value:** TV audiences can have higher expectations for ad production quality compared to digital platforms. At this stage, it may make sense to allocate more budget to refine the production quality of your winning YouTube ads.

Figure Out the Right Media Mix

Getting the right mix of TV and YouTube can have a dramatic impact for your brand. A study of three thousand ad campaigns found that 46 percent of them would have had an average of 42 percent more reach for the same budget had they added more YouTube advertising.[59] Nielsen TAR results, which measure the total reach and effectiveness of an advertisement across TV and digital, for Fiat Chrysler's Ram Trucks showed that 59 percent of people reached by YouTube in the twenty-five to fifty-four demographic were not reached by TV. Hershey's found that YouTube delivered ten times the reach efficiency of TV for their Reese's Christmas Trees campaign. And the AARP saw that 70 percent of their forty-five to sixty-four demographic reached on YouTube would not have been reached on TV, and YouTube's cost per reach was three times lower than TV.[60]

The following are a few ideas to help you optimize the mix of TV and digital advertising:

- **Get free reach for the same budget:** While reach is not the ultimate goal, getting more reach for free is very likely a good thing. As a first optimization step, find the mix of TV and YouTube that gives your brand the maximum reach for your current advertising budget. A great way to do that is by working with your Google team to do an Extra Reach analysis. I've seen many brands increase their reach by more than 30 percent, for the same advertising budget, by changing their media mix, almost always by adding more digital advertising.

- **Test with low-risk scenarios:** The analysis presented previously assumes that every point of reach has the same branding impact, which is clearly not the case. To optimize your media mix even further, it's important to test different media mixes and evaluate their impact on metrics like consideration lift and brand search lift.

  John Tuchtenhagen, head of media at Google for North America, recommends to "start with a low-risk scenario. Is there a particular day of the week, or week of the year, or type of campaign that tends not to perform well, despite media support? Try going dark on TV and shifting spend to digital video for that day or week or campaign. See what you learn from this new digital strategy and go from there."[61]

- **Try extreme tests:** After conducting some low-risk tests, I suggest also experimenting with extreme tests, where you explore radically different media mixes across various regions. In my experience, many companies have discovered that their media mix was completely misaligned through this kind of testing.

The US Navy tested a media mix of 100 percent digital and 0 percent TV for the first time. The campaign had incredible results: "People who saw the ads two or more times were 16 percent more likely to consider joining the US Navy, and users who saw the ads at least twice were 19 percent more likely to search for US Navy keywords on YouTube within three days." After this success, the Navy moved its media mix from 70 percent TV to 70 percent digital.[62]

The Oklahoma Tourism and Recreation Department increased traffic to its website (a good indicator of more travel to the state) by 500 percent without increasing their advertising budget by testing different mixes of TV and YouTube advertising in different states to determine their optimal media mix.[63]

- **Use light TV viewers targeting:** If you choose to shift your media mix from TV to YouTube, a smart approach could be to reallocate your lowest-performing TV investment, something your Google team can help you identify, to YouTube, specifically targeting light TV viewers who are interested in your product category. A pet food company might focus on consumers who have a pet but don't watch much TV.

Be Always On

After all this effort, something remarkable should be happening: a lot more searches for your brand, improved brand metrics, higher conversion rates on your website, and, ultimately, a significant increase in profits. Over time, these gains should translate into a noticeable increase in CLV.

But these gains can go away if you treat brand advertising as a temporary campaign with a beginning and an end. Instead, the strategy should focus on being always on, maintaining consistent brand advertising, with rapidly rotating creative, as long as it is financially sound.

Figure 5.6 shows that this fictitious company's brand searches are increasing by about 40 percent year-on-year (left axis) and that its cost to generate an additional brand search is around $1 (right axis). If this company has followed the previous steps, it may have concluded that maintaining a $1 (or lower) cost per additional brand search makes financial sense. While this remains true, the company should continue investing in brand advertising.

FIGURE 5.6 A GREAT BRAND ADVERTISING DASHBOARD

Brand Searches

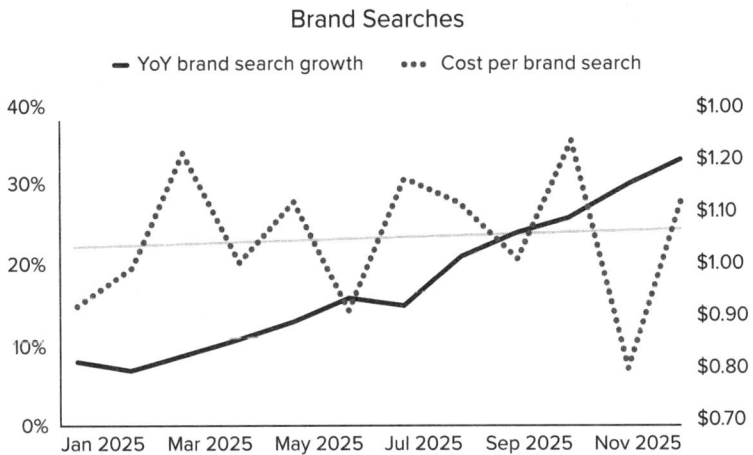

STEP 5—OPTIMIZE BRAND AND PERFORMANCE TOGETHER

Airbnb has recently downsized its performance marketing strategy to focus on big, bold branding efforts.[64] While it's great that Airbnb wants to tell a powerful brand story that will differentiate it from other lodging options, it shouldn't do it at the expense of its performance marketing investment. Assuming that Airbnb's performance marketing investment was profitable, why would they cut it in order to "afford" to do brand advertising?

What Airbnb should do instead is budget performance and brand advertising separately. Its performance advertising budget should be flexible and optimized to maximize net CLV (as per figure 2.3). Its brand advertising budget should also be flexible and increased only if more investment can increase brand metrics or brand searches at an acceptable price per increase (as per figure 5.6).

For example, education company MasterClass added a YouTube brand advertising campaign to its existing performance campaign. MasterClass's branding videos were targeted based on users' interests. If someone was looking for gardening tips, they would be served a MasterClass ad offering a course on gardening. This approach significantly boosted brand awareness and increased sign-ups by 70 percent.[65]

6

DELIVER AN EXCEPTIONAL
CUSTOMER EXPERIENCE

S equoias reach their full potential only in the right environment. They need fertile soil, lots of water, and the right climate to grow tall and strong. Similarly, corporate sequoias know that they must create an exceptional customer experience (CX) for customers to reach their full CLV potential.

Today's consumers, trained on amazing experiences from the likes of Amazon, Uber, and Netflix, expect their interactions with all companies to be seamless, fast, and personalized. In fact, Salesforce's *State of the Connected Customer* report, which surveyed fifteen thousand customers and business buyers globally, highlights that 84 percent of customers say the CX a company provides is as important as its products and services.[1]

Failing to meet customer expectations can have significant consequences. According to a PwC study, 32 percent of customers will stop buying from a brand they love after just one negative experience, while 92 percent would abandon the brand after two or three.[2] In the B2B sector, an Accenture study found that 44 percent of B2B buyers have switched vendors due to poor CX.[3]

If your CX is subpar, it's going to be much harder for you to acquire high-CLV customers and increase their CLV over time. As discussed in chapter 3, if a competitor generates 15 percent more profit (or CLV) per visit to their website or app because of a better CX, they will be able to invest 15 percent more to acquire each customer. Therefore, their digital ads will be displayed more frequently and prominently on all digital ad platforms. As a result, they will acquire a lot more customers (around 40 percent more in my experience), including more high-CLV customers. And as they test new ideas to increase the CLV of existing customers, every action they take will yield 15 percent more CLV, compounding their advantage.

Conversely, CX leaders thrive. A McKinsey study suggests that, between 2016 and 2021, companies leading in CX achieved more than double the revenue growth (no word on profit or CLV) compared to CX laggards.[4]

DIGITAL COMPANIES HAVE
BETTER CX, AND THE GAP IS WIDENING

Digital companies consistently achieve higher CX scores in most industries.[5] For example, Bain & Company found that online banks boast an average net promoter score of 34, significantly higher than the 18 scored by traditional banks.[6] E-commerce companies achieve an average satisfaction score of 80 versus 75 for department stores.[7] In insurance, only 5 percent of traditional insurers deliver the best-in-class CX offered by leading insurtech firms.[8] For example, Bestow allows customers to purchase up to $1 million in term life insurance online in less than five minutes, with no medical exam required. This level of convenience is almost unheard of among traditional insurers, many of which rely on in-person sales, lengthy application processes, and detailed health assessments.

The CX gap between digital and traditional companies is widening. A Gartner report found that 89 percent of digital companies reported significant improvements in customer satisfaction, versus 58 percent of traditional companies.[9] And according to Deloitte's 2022 *Digital Transformation Survey*, 70 percent of digital companies increased their CX technology investments, compared to 40 percent of traditional companies.[10]

Part of the reason for this widening gap is that digital-first companies tend to adopt the latest CX technologies faster. Research by McKinsey shows that companies that are in the top decile in the speed of their adoption of new digital technologies capture up to 80 percent of the digital revenues (no word on profits or CLV) in their industries.

These first-movers also achieve significantly higher shareholder returns. For example, insurance technology leaders have improved total shareholder returns 6.1 times more than laggards from 2018 to 2022. In CPG and retail, it's 2.9 times, and in energy and materials it's 2.3 times. In the retail banking industry, leading institutions generate an average of 70 percent of their total sales through digital channels, compared to just 17 percent for laggards. This digital advantage translates into superior financial performance, with leaders achieving a compound annual growth rate of 8.1 percent in total shareholder return, significantly outpacing the 4.9 percent CAGR of laggards.[11]

The technology adoption gap between first-movers and others continues to grow. From 2022 to 2024, the gap in digital and AI maturity has grown by 60 percent, as measured by McKinsey's Digital Quotient and AI Quotient assessments.[12]

ASBURY IMPROVES CONSUMER SATISFACTION
SCORES BY 30 PERCENT AND REVENUES BY 22 PERCENT

Not every nondigital company is falling behind. Asbury Auto, a midsize car dealership group based in the southeastern United States, transformed itself from a traditional auto dealer into one of the most digitally advanced and customer-friendly dealership groups in the world. In fact, in 2024, they were named one of the most trusted companies in the US by *Newsweek*, not an easy feat for a car dealership.

Notably, they became, to my knowledge, the first company in North America to sell cars entirely online. Customers can visit Asbury's website, Clicklane.com, and complete a legally binding car purchase, trade in their vehicle at a guaranteed price, secure financing with real-time offers from more than eighty banks, and add supplemental insurance like tire and wheel coverage, all in under ten minutes.

Asbury's extraordinary transformation didn't happen overnight, nor did it begin with a vision to create a world-class online buying experience. It started with a new CEO inspiring employees to delight customers, leading to small initiatives like salespeople placing giant bows on newly sold cars.

Over time, Asbury's growing CX successes inspired confidence, encouraged more ambitious ideas, and led to larger investments. When Asbury started building Clicklane, they didn't even have an in-house software development team and had to build one from scratch. As they built Clicklane.com, Asbury took an iterative approach and built what it could, leaving the more complex issues for later.

In five years, Asbury's customer satisfaction scores rose by 30 percent, sales increased by 22 percent despite flat overall US car sales, and the cost of selling a car dropped by 75 percent.

WHY DO SO FEW COMPANIES HAVE AN EXCEPTIONAL CX?

If developing a great CX can lead to such amazing results, why do so many companies struggle to improve it? Over the years, I've heard many reasons.

Our CX Is Already Great

A study found that 80 percent of business leaders rated their CX as exceptional, while only 20 percent of customers shared this sentiment.[13] This gap underscores the importance of judging the quality of a company's CX using actual customer feedback or third-party assessment.

And even if your CX is great, it can get better. First Direct, the online banking division of HSBC, was ranked number one in KPMG's *Customer Experience Excellence Report* in 2023 and has an NPS of 66, one of the highest in banking.[14] One of the main reasons is the average call waiting time of just thirty-nine seconds, compared to the industry average of more than eight minutes.[15] But instead of resting on its laurels, First Direct continues to improve its CX. Recently, the bank introduced a personalized digital financial adviser to promote each client's financial well-being. And First Direct's CEO, Chris Pitt, still calls every customer who recently had a bad customer experience with the bank.[16]

Our Competitors Don't Have a Good CX Either

Perfect. It should therefore be easy to steal their high-CLV customers if you can deliver a better CX. Moreover, your benchmark shouldn't be limited to local competitors; it should be to match the best CX within your industry globally or, even better, the best CX in any industry.

New Digital Companies Have Great CX but Are Losing Money

Many traditional companies dismiss digital-first new entrants because the new entrant is unprofitable. Regardless of their economics, if the new entrant has a better CX, it can change customer expectations significantly. Traditional companies should not emulate the CX innovations of digital-first entrants because of fear the new entrant will take over but because it can help them seize the advantage over their more traditional competitors.

Our Customers Don't Want a New CX

A common pitfall for some companies is falling into a self-fulfilling cycle where a bad CX masks latent customer demand for a better CX. I met the CEOs of many Canadian retailers over the years who were adamant that their customers were not interested in shopping online. They based this belief on the fact that a very small percentage of their company's sales were online. I tried to make the point that their website experiences were poor and showed data that online sales in the same category in the US were much higher and growing rapidly. But my points often fell on deaf ears.

When Amazon started investing more heavily in Canada, e-commerce grew quickly. This created the "Amazon Effect," a complete reset of customer expectations in Canada. Since they had not taken e-commerce seriously until then, some Canadian retailers struggled to compete.

Our Channel Partners Won't Like This

Some companies hesitate to improve their direct-to-customer CX out of fear it might create channel conflicts. While managing sales channels is very important, so is prioritizing customer needs. A Deloitte study found that customer-focused businesses are 60 percent more profitable than those that prioritize other stakeholders, demonstrating the tangible value of putting customers first.[17]

When it became clear that customers in the US wanted to buy car insurance online, some agent-led insurance companies hesitated, fearing backlash from their agents. Others transitioned to a hybrid model, giving customers the choice between buying online or buying through an agent. The really clever ones found a way to even make this transition appealing to agents by sending them high-quality leads for free.

As the agents got more leads, their business grew and their marketing costs declined, increasing profits. Over time, as the proportion of direct sales increased, some agents began to express dissatisfaction and became more concerned about channel conflict. But by then, the insurance company had gained significant leverage, and it was harder for the agents to exert pressure. In my experience, there's often a way to improve CX while making other sales channels happy, at least in the short term.

CX Improvements Are Too Expensive and Too Risky

Many executives are rightly taken aback when they see the investment suggested by the IT, marketing, and data sciences team to improve CX. In fact, International Data Corporation projected that global digital transformation spending would reach $3.9 trillion in 2027.[18]

McKinsey also points out that digital transformations can be risky. The average digital transformation has a 45 percent chance of delivering less profit than expected and only a 10 percent chance of exceeding profit expectations.[19]

But you should not let the high cost and risk deter you from starting or accelerating a CX journey because many improvements require minimal investment. You can kick off CX initiatives with simple ideas, just as Asbury did, and adopt an incremental approach.

We Don't Have Digital Expertise

Asbury did not have any digital experience when it started its CX improvements. And they built Clicklane without the latest AI tools that can help companies generate software much more easily and inexpensively than before.

A FIVE-STEP PROCESS TO
IMPROVE CX QUICKLY AND INEXPENSIVELY

Many companies have revolutionized their CX and reaped the rewards. In the hospitality industry, Hilton Hotels has set a benchmark with its Hilton Honors app, enabling guests to check in digitally, select their preferred rooms, and use their smartphones as room keys. Leveraging data analytics, Hilton also personalizes guest services and offers, delivering a highly tailored and convenient experience. These digital innovations have significantly increased customer satisfaction and loyalty, as reflected in Hilton's NPS of 17 compared to the industry average of 7.[20]

In the food and beverage industry, Domino's and Starbucks have set new standards in CX. Domino's launched its "Anyware" ordering platform, which allows customers to order in fifteen different ways, including through social media platforms, Amazon's Alexa, or Apple Smartwatch. It then uses the data to personalize every interaction based on previous purchases, optimize its digital advertising, streamline its supply chain, and make better menu decisions.

Similarly, Starbucks has transformed customer engagement through its app, which combines mobile ordering, personalized offers, and a robust loyalty program. In the new version of the app, customers can see the exact progress of their order and an estimate of when it will be ready. The app, with more than thirty-four million active users in the US, accounts for more than 31 percent of Starbucks' sales. Customers have also added more than $2 billion of funds in the Starbucks app.[21]

CX is improving rapidly in health care. For example, during a recent visit, my doctor used an AI system, with my consent, to take detailed notes, including complex medical terminology. At the end of the visit, the doctor showed me the transcript, and I was impressed. The AI had not only transcribed our conversation perfectly, even removing the extraneous chitchat, but also added structured data to my electronic health record. It also provided a differential diagnosis, which my doctor confirmed. The AI system also recommended the right medication. The prescription was then sent to my pharmacy automatically and delivered to my home the next day.

The doctor also explained that all she had to do was buy one piece of software. While it wasn't inexpensive, she shared that it saved her five to eight minutes per appointment. Her income had increased significantly as a result since she could see more patients. She was also adamant that, even with the increased patient load, the quality of care had improved because she could focus almost entirely on practicing medicine rather than dealing with paperwork.

To help you achieve similar results, the following is a low-risk and cost-effective five-step process to improve your CX.

STEP 1—START WITH THE RIGHT KPIS

What website page would you prefer your customers see? Page A that converts them into buyers at a rate of 2.5 percent or Page B that converts them at 2 percent?

By now, I'm sure you know the answer: There's not enough information to decide. What if Page A converts at a higher rate but leads to a basket size that is 30 percent lower? What if Page A offers more discounts than Page B so the margins are lower?

What if Page A converts the average customer better than Page B but performs worse with high-CLV customers? Relying on averages to test CX ideas can lead a company astray because the preferences of high-CLV customers may differ significantly from those of the average customer.

For example, Amazon data likely showed that a small percentage of customers accounted for a significant portion of profits and that these high-CLV customers valued fast delivery over price, while other customers were more price sensitive. To cater to these high-CLV customers,

Amazon launched Prime in 2005, offering free two-day shipping and exclusive benefits. Had Amazon focused on the average customer, it may never have even tested Amazon Prime.

Similarly, in B2B, companies should not build website pages that generate higher lead conversion rates. Page A might produce ten leads out of a hundred visits, for a 10 percent conversion rate, but none of those leads turn into paying customers. On the other hand, Page B might generate just eight leads out of a hundred visits, with an 8 percent conversion rate, but two of those leads turn into large paying customers.

Conversion rate, like ROAS or customer acquisition cost / CLV, is not a great metric, yet almost all website and app testing relies almost exclusively on it. Instead, when it comes to CX testing, I recommend using the same metric we covered in chapter 4, the change in CLV. And to ensure that CX changes don't increase CLV at the expense of customer satisfaction, I also recommend tracking the change in NPS (or another customer satisfaction metric) as a guardrail metric.

For existing customers, follow the process described in chapter 4, but with high-CLV customers: Create a test and control group of high-CLV customers, measure CLV and NPS before, use email to send the two groups to two different landing pages, and measure CLV and NPS again later. The winning page increased CLV per customer the most, without lowering NPS.

For new customers, use tools like Similar Audiences and Lookalikes to find prospective customers similar to your high-CLV customers, send them to two different landing pages, and evaluate which landing page has the highest total CLV per visitor, the CLV forecast of each new customer acquired divided by the number of visitors to that page. If possible, take a quick postconversion survey and compare the customer satisfaction of both pages to make sure the winning page doesn't generate lower customer satisfaction.

But be cautious: Testing new ideas with high-CLV customers can be riskier, because a poorly executed test can have greater financial consequences. If the test you're running is high risk, consider running it on average-CLV customers first.

If measuring the change in CLV is not feasible, a good proxy is profit per visit. While this metric measures only the short-term impact of a test, it's still better than conversion rate. As a last option, you can use the conversion rate of high-CLV customers.

To ensure improvements in conversion rates of high-CLV customers don't come at the cost of profitability, avoid using any discounting or giveaways in CX tests. Instead, test pricing and discounting strategies separately to isolate their effects from results driven solely by improved CX.

In some cases, it's impossible to measure the change in CLV or even the conversion rate. In these cases, use the best metric you can. Asbury selected their Google review score as their core metric. They chose their Google reviews because they're updated in real time, unlike metrics like the Customer Satisfaction Index score, a standard metric in the car dealership industry, which take months. Enterprise Rent-A-Car, as we will cover in chapter 7, chose a modified version of NPS as its core metric to measure all of its CX improvements, with great success.

STEP 2—UNDERSTAND WHAT HIGH-CLV CUSTOMERS WANT

To improve the CX for high-CLV customers, it's essential to identify what drives their buying decisions and what improvements they would expect your company to make. Below are some techniques to get more in-depth information about what high-CLV customers want.

Goals Assessment

Some research, from books like *The Effortless Experience*[22] and companies like ChurnRX, suggests that there is a low correlation between customer satisfaction and loyalty. Instead, what matters most is helping customers achieve great results, which can increase retention by six- to tenfold.[23]

It's therefore critical to understand the goals customers want to achieve. In the B2B world, this can mean understanding what KPIs a company wants to improve, not what features they want. To do this, it's important to ask questions like, "What are the two or three metrics you'd like to see improve as you use our product/service?"

In the B2C world, it can mean better understanding the "job to be done," the underlying objective the customer is trying to accomplish. For example, this may mean Nike understanding that high-CLV customers don't want to buy athletic gear; they want to achieve a wellness goal.

Data Analytics

You can generate great insights about high-CLV customers by looking at data. The Very group, a leading UK e-commerce retailer, wanted to acquire more of what it calls its "bullseye" customers, a high-CLV segment. By digging deeper into their data they found that, counterintuitively, customers that financed their purchase instead of paying for them up front were much more valuable. Using this insight, they were able to predict in advance which customers were more likely to finance their purchase and acquire more of them.[24]

Churn Analysis

Another way to better understand what high-CLV customers want is by analyzing what they don't want. To do that, map the historical causes of churn of previous high-CLV customers using surveys and customer service records. Then add the total CLV lost for each reason of churn.

You can now assess what issues cause the most total loss in CLV and try to reverse them.

Search Behavior

Using Google tools like Customer Match, you can identify what your high-CLV customers are searching for to understand what is top of mind for them in real time.

Marketing Data

I've worked with many companies that gained deeper insights into their high-CLV customers by using marketing tools like Google's Audience Manager and Affinity Audiences. Using these tools, a company could discover that their most valuable customers tend to be female, between the ages of forty and fifty-six, have a higher likelihood of being parents, are actively searching for pet products, sports equipment, and a vacation home, and enjoy going to museums, investing, and antiquing.

Customer Journey Mapping and Ethnographic Research

While analytics provide quantitative insights, many companies complement them with qualitative research. Customer journey mapping breaks down every interaction, from discovery to purchase to support, to identify where high-CLV customers see value or encounter friction. Some AI tools can now map customer journeys in near–real time to help companies improve CX faster.

Ethnographic research involves shadowing customers in their day-to-day lives or observing how they use a product at home or work. This method can reveal needs customers may not explicitly state.

Sephora's innovation lab used in-store observations, journey mapping, and interviews with top Beauty Insider members to understand how they engaged with products, displays, and staff, revealing that high-CLV customers craved guided, educational encounters rather than just more merchandise or discounts. This led Sephora to introduce personalized tutorials, hands-on learning stations, and augmented reality (AR) try-on tools.[25]

Airbnb's Snow White Project, inspired by Walt Disney's use of storyboarding to craft immersive narratives, helped Airbnb visualize forty-five key CX moments, like planning a trip with a friend, searching for the right accommodation, booking the trip, pretrip contact with the host, getting the Wi-Fi password, getting the keys, and so on. To complement this storyboarding, Airbnb conducted ethnographic research, immersing themselves in the lives of their users by staying in properties as guests, interviewing top-performing hosts, and observing how high-CLV users interacted with the platform.

This qualitative research uncovered functional issues like confusing navigation and emotional barriers such as trust and communication hesitancy. The insights led to impactful design changes, such as improving messaging tools, refining search filters, enhancing customer support, and adding trust-building features like verified profiles.[26]

Voice of the Customer Programs

Voice-of-the-customer (VoC) programs are structured initiatives designed to gather direct feedback from customers. VoC initiatives often include tools like surveys, focus groups, customer advisory boards, and online forums.

Most companies have a VoC program, but few do it well, surveying random customers instead of surveying high-CLV customers and segmenting them into more granular groups to understand the needs of each microsegment. Advanced survey tools like Alida and Fuel Cycle help build, maintain, and survey engaged communities and can help gather insights about high-CLV microsegments and provide longitudinal data to understand how these customers' needs evolve over time.[27]

Other tactics include triggering website or app surveys for high-CLV customers taking specific actions (for example, abandoning a cart with specific products in it, hovering over a certain part of a website, or taking too long to complete a task). You can even link these surveys to your marketing and website analytics to better understand the impact of survey answers on purchases and other important website metrics by marketing channel.

Using these techniques, Dick's Sporting Goods learned that customers going directly to their website behaved very differently than customers coming from a Google Ad and created a different merchandising strategy for each, leading to a significant decrease in cart abandonments.[28]

Cocreation Programs

Another powerful approach is to give high-CLV customers a direct voice in CX improvements by inviting them into private advisory groups, beta testing communities, or cocreation workshops.

DHL uses cocreation sessions at its innovation centers, inviting top customers to collaborate in identifying supply chain pain points and testing new logistics technologies. Due to these joint development sessions, DHL improved delivery accuracy, shortened response times, and increased overall customer satisfaction scores by 80 percent, which led to higher retention rates and profit growth among its most valuable clients.[29]

Cocreation can be greatly accelerated by using digital technologies. IKEA introduced its digital "Co-Create IKEA" platform, inviting customers, entrepreneurs, students, and innovation labs worldwide to contribute product ideas online. By offering resources like prototype shops, running virtual boot camps, and providing cash incentives and licensing deals, IKEA has helped customers generate thousands of new product ideas.[30]

Academic Research

There is a lot of research on the CX priorities of high-CLV customers in multiple industries. Using powerful AI tools like Consensus, you can easily find and access this information. An academic paper shows that there are four elements to Airbnb's CX that matter most to frequent customers: home-like comfort, amenities, and security; personalized services with tailored interactions and host engagement; authentic experiences through immersion in local culture; and social interactions that foster connections between hosts, guests, and fellow travelers.[31]

While understanding the needs of high-CLV customers is very important, anticipating them is even better. Some companies can predict customer needs at the individual customer level and act on those predictions in real time. As McKinsey describes it, "One leading airline built a machine-learning system . . . to measure both satisfaction and predicted revenue for its more than 100 million customers every day. The system allowed the airline to identify and prioritize those customers whose relationships were most at risk because of a delay or cancellation and offer them personalized compensation to save the relationship and reduce customer defection on high-priority routes . . . which resulted in an 800 percent uplift in satisfaction and a 60 percent reduction in churn for priority customers."[32]

Whatever tools you use to better understand high-CLV customers, it's also important to share what you've learned with them, so they feel heard. For example, SugarCRM gathers regular customer feedback using multiple tools and follows up with every customer who shares input. They also created SugarClub, a platform to communicate with users and share updates on how feedback is being addressed.

STEP 3—START NOW WITH SMALL IMPROVEMENTS

In the introduction, I promised strategies that don't rely on costly technology investments. While some CX initiatives involve significant costs and risks, as we'll discuss later, many companies start their CX transformation with simple, low-cost changes that can deliver quick, significant results. Many companies tackle these changes by starting a small cross-functional CX team, a simple solution that sidesteps the need for a broader cultural overhaul of the entire company to focus on customer-centricity.

Asbury started with putting giant bows on newly sold cars. Asbury then dealt with important but fairly easy-to-address issues like decreasing the time it took to do oil changes. After management spotted negative reviews at multiple dealerships that oil changes took more than four hours, they sent a team to these dealerships to analyze the process and make recommendations. Based on these findings, Asbury built a simple electronic job-dispatching system that reduced oil change times to under an hour by allocating labor more efficiently.

Next, Asbury found that customers were very skeptical about inspections because they felt that there were too many recommendations of things to fix during routine inspections. Asbury tested numerous ideas in multiple dealers. The winning idea was simple: taking a video of the recommended repairs and sending it to customers who can thumbs-up or thumbs-down the recommended fix and then pay for the repairs automatically inside the Asbury app. This relatively simple fix increased customer service scores and also increased the average repair bill by 50 percent as customers better understood repair recommendations.

The following are some suggestions to help you get more CX wins more quickly.

Avoid Overplanning

Instead of developing complex road maps or striving for perfection, focus on continuous improvement. This approach emphasizes addressing immediate, solvable issues and deferring more complex challenges until the foundational work is in place.

Asbury faced significant challenges in selling cars online, including having to provide real-time, accurate trade-in valuations and maintaining precise pricing and inventory data across all dealerships. While some dealership groups still allow these complexities to stall their digital transformation, Asbury focused on addressing manageable issues first while deferring more complex problems for later.

Don't Wait for a Perfect Understanding of Customers

Some companies look for a "perfect" understanding of customers before improving their CX. This strategy often fails for three reasons:

1. First, customer journeys are now very complex and change quickly. I've met many companies that had mapped hundreds of unique customer journeys over years but had not improved any of them.

2. Second, waiting for perfect insights will inevitably lead to missed opportunities. One company Neil Hoyne advised spent three years and more than $200 million to build a cloud-based customer data platform (CDP). Unfortunately, by the time the project was completed, customer expectations had shifted dramatically, reducing the value of the investment. Meanwhile, their CX remained stagnant, with few improvements made during this long project.

3. Third, most large projects to better understand customers fail. According to Gartner, fewer than 10 percent of companies have successfully established a 360-degree customer view, and only

about 5 percent are able to use this view to systematically grow their businesses.[33]

Instead of looking for a "perfect" understanding of customers, focus on making incremental improvements to known pain points. Before it has developed a full understanding of why customers abandon a shopping cart, an e-commerce company could improve a high cart abandonment rate by testing simple fixes like prominently displaying estimated delivery dates during checkout.

Focus on a Few Customer Journeys

For most companies, a few customer journeys have the greatest influence on high-CLV customers. In retail banking, the top three journeys (transparency in prices and fees, ease of communication with the bank, and keeping track of the status of the account-opening process) account for 40 percent of the entire customer satisfaction rating.[34]

While key customer journeys vary across industries, there are several common themes. In the B2C sector, nearly 80 percent of American consumers identify speed, convenience, expert assistance, and friendly service as the most crucial factors contributing to a positive CX.[35]

Focusing on a few important customer journeys can make a big difference. A global CPG company shifted from scattered efforts across two hundred pilots to prioritizing three, which were successful, and added a 15–20 percent increase in digital maturity and more than $400 million in earnings before interest and taxes in three years.[36]

Prioritize Known Winners

In nearly every industry, there's a well-defined set of CX improvements that deliver the greatest impact. Every senior executive in your company should be familiar with these. To build that list, do a worldwide competitive analysis to uncover the top CX innovations in your industry, create a thorough inventory of trusted software providers offering CX tools in your industry and map the improvements they provide, and add the strategies outlined next, which tend to work in many industries.

Improve the Communication of Your Value Proposition

Some companies achieve substantial improvements in key metrics like CSAT, NPS, and CLV by effectively communicating the value proposition their customers are already receiving.

GiveDirectly, a nonprofit organization that facilitates direct cash transfers to individuals living in extreme poverty, asks donors visiting its website to subscribe to its newsletter. GiveDirectly knows that a donor that subscribes has a significantly higher CLV. By simply changing the text beside the newsletter subscription checkbox from "Sign up for our newsletter" to "Stay informed about the impact of your donation (1–3 emails/mo)," GiveDirectly doubled the percentage of donors who subscribed from 25 percent to 50 percent.[37]

Nail Onboarding

In B2B SaaS, poor onboarding generates 23 percent of churn.[38] The same is true in many other industries. To reduce churn resulting from inadequate onboarding, create a seamless, informative, and personalized onboarding experience that helps customers quickly understand and appreciate the value of your product or service. This can be achieved through clear communication, interactive tutorials, and proactive follow-ups to address any questions or concerns.

Instead of a canned demo, first-time users of Canva are asked what they will use it for and get a personalized onboarding based on that main use case. HubSpot, Gusto, and many modern SaaS tools provide new users a checklist they must perform, at their own pace, to get full value from the product.[39] Seventy-five percent of users say video is the best way to learn a new product.[40] Toggl takes video demos to the next level by creating tens of small explanation videos that are played at the right time, instead of one large video demo. And StoryChief weaves customer testimonials into its demo videos.[41] Other ideas include adding an interactive guide to help new users at every step, showing the benefit to the user of taking a certain step, using templates to accelerate the time-to-value, and popping up a helpbot when a user seems stuck.

ZoomInfo has an award-winning onboarding process. One of the most important things they did is extend their onboarding from thirty to ninety days: "In the first 30 days, customers focus on planning, technical setup, and education, setting the foundation for a successful onboarding journey. This initial stage includes a kickoff call, system integration led by Technical Implementation Managers, and tailored training sessions. The final 60 days are dedicated to driving product adoption, which is critical for value realization and customer retention."[42]

Improve Speed

If the speed of your mobile site improves by just 0.1 seconds, it will generate on average 8 percent more revenue per visit (no information on profit or CLV).[43] A simple but effective way to increase site speed is to segment users based on their connection speed and deliver lower resolution images to those on slow connections. There are many other ways to generate small improvements in speeds, like compressing images and using a content delivery network.

A more comprehensive but more complex strategy is to use progressive web application (PWA) technologies. Alibaba already had a high-performing mobile site, but when it implemented PWA, conversion rates (no word on profit or CLV) improved 76 percent.[44] Spotify used PWA to increase one-day plays by 54 percent and app downloads by 31 percent. While shifting to a PWA website may be expensive, in my experience, it usually pays for itself fairly quickly. Before you make that investment, do a simple test. Purposely slow down your website speed by a few tenths of a second for a small percentage of your users and evaluate the loss in CLV. This will help you somewhat predict the value of a PWA investment.

Simplify

Many customers, especially high-CLV customers, want to get a job done and move on. This is why simplicity is often key in CX. An excellent way to reimagine your CX is to start with the simplest possible way for a customer to accomplish their primary tasks, in theory, whether it's practical or not. From there, incorporate only features that are absolutely essential or add significant value.

Consider how effortless it would be if a driver could get car insurance simply by taking a photo of their driver's license. The insurance company could extract the necessary information from the license and augment it with third-party data. Some additional data might improve risk-assessment and quote accuracy, but it would be worth testing the trade-off between a more accurate quote and a dramatically simpler process. Imagine the power of an ad campaign like "Ten seconds can save you 15 percent." While this may not be feasible due to legal or technological constraints, it should be the starting point of any process simplification efforts. Additional friction should be introduced only if it's necessary.

HotelTonight revolutionized hotel booking by prioritizing simplicity and efficiency. With their app, I was able to book a room in just four taps and eight seconds, significantly faster than the forty-two taps and ninety-nine seconds it took me on a competing app. To achieve this great CX, HotelTonight focused on an unconventional KPI for online travel agencies: time to book. By analyzing competitors' apps, they identified steps that created customer friction, like account creation requirements, and eliminated them.[45]

Similarly, Uber asks only for a phone number to create an account. Features like trip histories, saved payment methods, and personalized recommendations are gradually introduced, but only after the core experience, booking a ride, is made seamless.

Domino's outdid Amazon's one-click buy when they launched zero-click ordering. Customers could reorder their favorite pizza by simply opening the Domino's app and waiting ten seconds, at which time their pizza would be ordered automatically and delivered a few minutes later.

International Game Technology recently rolled out a technology for cashless slot machines. Casino customers don't need to insert cash or a credit card into a slot machine. They simply link their bank account to their casino loyalty card and can access limitless cash with a simple tap.[46]

York Minster, formerly the Cathedral of Saint Peter, in York, England, offers the congregation the opportunity to give to the church in denominations of five pounds and ten pounds by contactless card donations while still maintaining the look of the donation plate. This strategy has led to 97 percent more donations.[47]

Expedia removed the optional "company" field on its checkout page because it confused customers, with many entering their bank's name and address, causing credit card verification failures. This simple change increased Expedia's profits by $12 million.[48]

Staples transformed its guest checkout process by reducing the number of inputs from twenty-two to just five, resulting in a 50 percent reduction in checkout time and a significant boost in conversions (no information on profit or CLV). The company consolidated fields, such as combining "Street Address," "City," "State," and "ZIP" into a single "Shipping Address" field, and implemented smart tools like the Google Maps API for auto-complete. Staples also simplified inputs by defaulting billing addresses to match shipping addresses, using inline email validation, and allowing all credit card details to be entered on one line with fields adapting to the card type.[49]

The LVMH fashion brand Loro Piana unveiled Silhouette, an interactive display that allows users to create a digital avatar of themselves and style it in virtual Loro Piana garments. This innovation offers customers a modern try-before-you-buy experience from anywhere, helping customers try hundreds of outfits quickly.

In B2B, 60–70 percent of buyers prefer self-service over talking to a sales representative.[50] As a result, they are increasingly rejecting traditional gated-content approaches, where companies require them to share personal information before they can access meaningful resources. Instead, they expect transparency and immediate access to key information, such as product demo videos, case studies, white papers, pricing, and important features.

This doesn't mean you should ungate all your content. Instead, experiment with different versions of your site and identify the strategy that drives the highest CLV. If measuring CLV isn't possible, focus on the best available proxy, such as the pipeline generated by each page or, as a simpler but less effective alternative, the number of demo requests each page generates. But avoid defaulting to the page that produces the most leads, as previously discussed, since lead quantity isn't the same as lead quality. Dynamic Yield tested different options and found that, for them, the best approach was to ungate all their case studies but add a demo request form at the bottom of each.[51]

When buyers are ready to engage, why not give them multiple options, like an AI chatbot to answer basic questions, a video chat with a human that can be activated immediately, or a meeting with a sales representative that can be booked directly from your site in a few seconds using Calendly?

Personalize

A study by Google suggests that customers who can find the right information personalized for them are 3.2 times more likely to buy from and eighteen times more likely to recommend a brand.[52] A Boston Consulting Group study suggests that retailers using best practices in personalization see up to 400 percent sales lift and 40 percent higher average order value (no information on profits or CLV).[53]

Lack of personalization can not only disappoint customers; it can dramatically lower a company's profits. For example, retailers that don't personalize their e-commerce site will necessarily show similar products to every customer. Typically, they showcase the most popular products, the ones customers click on the most. While this approach might seem logical, it can significantly lower margins, because the products customers click on the most are often heavily discounted, low margin products. In addition, if all customers see similar products, they will never see the majority of other products in the same category, eventually forcing the retailer to mark down prices of these products too.

Amazon addresses this challenge by using AI to personalize every shopping experience using a customer's previous purchase history and their real-time browsing behavior, ensuring that customers get a deeply personalized experience whether they are logged in or logged out.

To try to approximate Amazon's sophisticated recommendation system, some retailers use manual rules-based systems. Merchants input complex sets of rules, sometimes numbering in the tens of thousands, to dictate which products are shown to which customers (for example, show fewer winter clothes to customers in Miami). This method has many limitations:

- It only works for customers that are logged in, and a high percentage of e-commerce sessions are logged out.

- These manual rules are created for large customer segments, so the personalization is not at the individual customer level.

- Managing thousands of rules is time consuming and prone to errors, making it difficult to scale effectively.

- Manual rules cannot adapt quickly to changing customer behaviors or market trends.

- Manual rules cannot optimize profits or CLV nearly as well as an AI system.

But many retailers, who are typically run by merchandisers, are not adapting. In fact, I met a senior retail executive in 2025 who told me that the reason they didn't use an AI recommendation system was that their merchants knew their customers more than AI. To which I replied, "All ten million of them?" The best e-commerce companies in the world use AI to do the grunt work of basic personalization and use experienced merchants to augment the system by testing hypotheses the AI would not test on its own, as described in chapter 4.

In B2B, buyers expect the same level of personalized experiences they receive as consumers. Salesforce's *State of the Connected Customer* report found that 72 percent of business buyers expect vendors to personalize engagement to their needs, and 69 percent are willing to pay more for a great experience.[54] McKinsey reports that B2B companies implementing personalization strategies have seen a 5–10 percent increase in revenue (no word on profits or CLV).[55]

The following are examples of personalization that had a big impact, starting with simple ideas that are inexpensive to test and execute.

- Sport Chek, Canada's largest sporting goods retailer, increased e-commerce revenues by 7.3 percent by personalizing its cart page (no word on profits or CLV). Instead of the usual "Shipping is free on orders over $25" message, Sport Chek tailored the message to each customer's individual situation. For example, a message that said "Congratulations, you qualify for free shipping" when customers met the free shipping criteria and a message that said "Order $25 more to qualify for free shipping" when they didn't.[56]

- Very, a UK fashion brand, increased profits significantly by personalizing landing pages and product recommendations based on each customer's local weather conditions.[57]

- Wider Funnel, a conversion-rate optimization company, tested a new landing page that decreased conversion rates by 8 percent (no word on profits or CLV). Instead of abandoning the test, they analyzed the data more in depth and found that the new page performed 24 percent better for older users but 38 percent worse for younger ones. They created multiple landing page variations for different age groups and significantly improved results.[58]

- Red Roof Inn created a system to monitor flight delays and target these travelers with real-time ads. Messages like "Stuck at JFK? Stay with us!" provided timely and relevant solutions for stranded passengers. This strategy resulted in a 60 percent increase in bookings from their search ads.[59]

- Waze saw an 865 percent increase in conversion rates (no word on profits or CLV) by exposing real-time traffic in their ads, allowing potential users to experience the power of Waze before downloading it.[60]

- Snowflake used Mutiny's personalization tools to streamline account-based marketing, segmenting content on its site by industry, account, and individual users. Personalized pages were four times more likely to generate a client meeting. Overall, Snowflake's personalization strategy resulted in the acquisition of more customers and an 80 percent increase in the average contract value of these customers.[61]

- Instacart's Ask Instacart AI tool, much like Amazon's Rufus, brings personalization to the next level by leveraging aggregated and anonymized data from more than one billion orders to power natural language search. Shoppers can receive recommendations on specific questions like "What's a healthy snack for a thirty-five-year-old vegan?"

STEP 4—MAKE BIGGER BETS

By focusing on smaller wins first, you'll be better positioned to tackle larger, more transformative initiatives. These bigger projects will feel less daunting because you'll have already built trust within your organization, gained confidence in your CX strategies, and generated some of the cash flow necessary to support more ambitious efforts.

I've seen many companies transition from achieving small CX wins to making bold, transformative changes. Here are some recommendations to help you make this shift effectively.

Prove the Financial Value of CX

Before making larger investments, it's important to prove the financial value of CX. This will help you convince internal and external stakeholders that this is a good idea. Surprisingly, only 4 percent of companies can calculate the financial impact of CX projects.[62]

If you've had some small CX wins, you should be able to at least loosely correlate a CX improvement metric (NPS, CSAT . . .) with a financial metric, ideally CLV, but if not, profits or revenues.

Wajax, a large industrial products distributor that does seven hundred thousand transactions per year, learned through a detailed analysis that NPS promoters spent twice as much as detractors. Using this data, Wajax built a simulator to show the financial impact of increasing NPS, resulting in significant internal buy-in for an investment to increase NPS, including a program to try to turn every detractor into a promoter by meeting every single one of them. Wajax's NPS has increased from 62 to 71 from 2019 to 2023.[63]

Start with Use Cases, Not Technology

Instead of starting with the technology (for example, we need a CDP), identify specific use cases that can drive meaningful impact. One of the reasons is that the view of the customer needed for every use case tends to be very different. For example, an email marketer needs to predict what a customer will want to buy next whereas a customer service agent needs to understand the return policies of previous products purchased.

If you decide to spend heavily on a new CX technology without first carefully considering the use cases, the chances of success are slim, in my experience.

As Esteban Kolsky, SAP Customer Experience's chief evangelist, says, instead of building a 360-degree view of the customer from the beginning, "the better strategy is to focus on use cases and figure out how to get the trusted, accurate, relevant, real-time customer data for those instances."[64]

American Eagle did it right. They knew they wanted to build a 360-degree view of the customer. But instead of doing this in a vacuum, they started with two use cases: personalizing website recommendations and emails. In partnership with Merkle, they first consolidated the data they needed for these use cases. These two use cases alone increased conversion rates by 400 percent and also significantly increased CLV, which they couldn't measure before. After this success, American Eagle kept adding more data to the 360-degree view of the customers to build more use cases.[65]

Adopt a Fast-Follower Strategy

To prioritize big bet use cases, adopt a fast-follower strategy of worldwide best practices. A bank in France shouldn't wait for other banks in France to improve their CX. Instead, it should adopt new ideas from other banking markets, like Switzerland, Singapore, China, the UK, and the US. It should know every new CX idea being deployed in those markets and deploy a new idea when there's just enough evidence that it is working in those markets, rather than waiting for perfect proof.

Leverage AI

If you're planning to take big bets, why not leapfrog directly to AI? When reimagining your CX, it's important to embrace ideas that were unimaginable until recently and approach the process with a blank slate.

Writing about AI in a book that will be published months from now is challenging. The rapidly evolving landscape risks making some observations outdated—but I will try to provide insights that remain relevant.

Despite some recent headlines that AI investments yield limited financial gains, McKinsey presents a brighter view. They note, "Although it is still early days, our experience shows that leveraging generative AI can significantly reduce manual work, accelerating tech modernization timelines by 40 to 50 percent, cutting technology debt costs by 40 percent, and simultaneously enhancing the quality of outputs."[66]

Generative AI use cases are exploding. Here are a few interesting ones:

- **Wendy's FreshAI:** Wendy's has introduced FreshAI, an AI assistant that takes orders at Wendy's drive-throughs. Wendy's says that FreshAI improves drive-through speed and accuracy, cutting time by twenty-two seconds with 86 percent accuracy, which grows to 99 percent with the help of humans.

- **Netflix trailers:** Netflix is testing generative AI to create personalized movie and show trailers tailored to individual user preferences, helping to increase engagement and content discovery.

- **NASA's mission simulations:** NASA uses generative AI to simulate space mission scenarios, including spacecraft designs and planetary explorations, allowing scientists to anticipate challenges and optimize mission outcomes before they happen.

- **Spotify playlists:** Spotify uses generative AI to create unique, mood-based playlists for users by analyzing their listening habits and even generating original AI-composed music to match specific vibes.

- **Game design:** Game studios are using generative AI to rapidly create entire virtual worlds, including terrain, characters, and storylines, cutting years off game development timelines while improving creativity.

The next evolution in CX beyond generative AI is likely to be agentic AI. This form of AI breaks down complex tasks into components and autonomously executes them on behalf of the user. Imagine receiving a wedding invitation. With the help of an advanced AI agent, you could scan the invitation, and the AI would seamlessly handle the logistics and decisions for you. It might automatically send an RSVP with perfect etiquette, book flights and hotels tailored to your preferences and loyalty programs, and select a thoughtful gift based on the couple's registry, personal tastes, and your budget.

The AI could go further, curating personalized outfit suggestions for every wedding-related event, such as the rehearsal dinner and wedding brunch, factoring in the dress code, your personal style, and current fashion trends. It could even schedule in-store or virtual fittings, arrange alterations where necessary, and ensure everything is ready in time.

While this vision may seem futuristic, many experts suggest that companies need to start preparing for this reality now. The emergence of agentic AI is likely to require a complete reimagining of the customer experience, moving from reactive interactions to proactive, autonomous systems that anticipate and resolve customer needs before they arise. Although this book will not delve into the intricacies of agentic AI, I encourage you to stay informed about advancements in this area. Keep an eye on emerging agentic AI software companies that are pushing the boundaries of what's possible in CX and be open to engaging in conversations with these innovators. If agentic AI looks promising by the time you read this, you might skip some of the earlier steps and leapfrog straight to using it.

Partner

Before starting costly IT projects or building your own generative or agentic AI solutions, partner with major AI companies like Google, Microsoft, or OpenAI and specialized vendors like chatbot or virtual shopping tool providers. These companies have invested tens of billions in advanced AI systems, and partnering with them can help you launch cutting-edge solutions faster and more affordably.

In customer service, there are existing tools that can:

Create incredible self-service CX: Using tools like retrieval-augmented generation, you can build a chatbot trained on your internal documents that delivers a ChatGPT-like conversational experience in multiple languages with a much lower likelihood of generating inaccurate responses ("hallucinations"). Some of these systems can also seamlessly handle customer queries across channels like phone, SMS, and email.

By integrating with AI avatar providers, you can even transform the chatbot from a text-based interface into an interaction with a highly realistic, humanlike avatar. AI systems can even sense emotion with high accuracy and reply with the appropriate response with the appropriate tone of voice based on the situation.

The latest systems promise chatbots that can perform tasks like opening a new account, without the need for complex back-end integration and the ability for chatbots to automatically cross-sell and upsell.

Revamp your call center CX: If self-service doesn't give a customer the answers they need, AI can also help improve the call center CX. Some software can instantly identify the customer, show their recent interactions with the self-service bot, and suggest solutions before the conversation begins. During the call, the AI transcribes in real time, spots key issues, and finds solutions automatically without the agent having to search for the answer. After each customer interaction, AI can create personalized follow-ups like confirmation emails, thank-you notes, or helpful resources based on the discussion.

Deliver proactive support: AI can analyze patterns in service tickets and customer interactions to predict problems and provide proactive solutions. GE HealthCare uses AI to monitor medical devices for signs of failure, allowing them to schedule repairs before customer service issues arise.

Consider Acquiring a Start-Up

For some companies, the quickest and best way to transform their CX is through acquisition. While specific advice depends on your situation, I recommend you stay closely connected with key innovative companies in your industry.

Under the leadership of Chief Digital Officer Lubomira Rochet and Global Chief Digital Marketing Officer Asmita Dubey, L'Oréal acquired ModiFace, a cutting-edge AR and AI beauty company. This acquisition became the backbone of several groundbreaking CXs like:

- **Virtual try-on tools:** Leveraging ModiFace's AR technology, L'Oréal developed features that allowed customers to virtually try on makeup and hair color products, enhancing online shopping experiences.

- **AI-powered beauty advisers:** Tools like Beauty Genius, a generative AI–powered consultant, and Skin Genius, a diagnostic tool that provides personalized skin care recommendations based on AI analysis of skin conditions, created deeply personalized customer interactions.

This acquisition sparked more innovation. Since then, L'Oréal has developed or acquired several outstanding products that greatly improve CX:

- **Color Sonic and Brow Magic:** L'Oréal recently launched Color Sonic, a handheld device powered by AI that enables customers to apply salon-quality hair color at home with ease. Similarly, Brow Magic offers personalized brow-mapping and application, helping customers achieve professional results using advanced AI and AR.

- **YSL Rouge Sur Mesure:** Yves Saint Laurent Rouge Sur Mesure is an AI-powered device that lets users create almost endless lipstick shades through an app. Customers can mix their own colors, match them perfectly to an outfit, and virtually try them on before applying.

- **Garnier Hair Color Services:** Garnier Hair Color Services is an app that helps customers find and virtually try on their perfect hair color using AI. It evaluates their hair type, desired results, and preferences to give personalized recommendations from Garnier's products.

Gopi Kallayil has collaborated with L'Oréal for years. He praised L'Oréal's digital transformation, saying, "L'Oréal has achieved one of the greatest digital transformations I've ever seen. What makes it so successful is that it's never been about technology; it's always been about crafting an exceptional customer experience."

John Deere, traditionally known for making tractors, made bold moves to become a tech leader in precision agriculture. Embracing AI, the company acquired Blue River Technology in 2017, a start-up specializing in computer vision and robotics for farming. By using computer vision, this technology identifies and targets weeds with remarkable precision, reducing herbicide use by up to 90 percent.[67] The system also collected a lot of data that John Deere used to provide farmers with valuable insights on soil conditions, weather patterns, and crop health.

Following the Blue River acquisition, John Deere made further strategic moves to transform itself from a tractor manufacturer to a farmer productivity company, by acquiring multiple AI and robotics companies, including:

- **Bear Flag Robotics:** Specializing in autonomous tractor technology, Bear Flag Robotics allowed John Deere to develop self-driving agricultural equipment that reduces labor costs and improves efficiency.

- **Harvest Profit:** A financial management software company that provided farmers with predictive tools to manage profitability and make data-driven decisions.

- **Operations Center:** A digital platform that integrates data from John Deere equipment, weather, soil, and satellite imagery to provide real-time insights into crop performance and operations. This platform allows farmers to optimize planting, fertilization, and harvesting decisions with unprecedented precision.

STEP 5—ROLL OUT CX
IMPROVEMENT ACROSS THE ORGANIZATION

At this stage, you should have a small, centralized CX team focused on achieving incremental CX wins, along with an IT team pursuing larger, transformative initiatives. The next step is to foster a company-wide culture of CX improvement, where every employee actively contributes to enhancing CX daily. Here's how Asbury accomplished it:[68]

- **Lead from the top:** In my experience, a company-wide shift to more customer centricity almost always begins at the top. The CEO must drive the vision, allocate necessary resources, and inspire the entire organization to embrace change. When David Hult became CEO at Asbury, he made CX the company's number one priority. This was a significant cultural shift from the previous sales-at-all-costs mentality. He explained, in almost every meeting he attended, that there was a direct correlation between the company's CX (as measured by the Google reviews of each of its dealers) and company profits. He then followed this talk with important actions. For example, he publicly rejected many ideas that could significantly lower costs but would also lower Google reviews.

- **Demonstrate 100 percent commitment:** David Hult was also very clear, from the beginning, that employees who didn't buy into the vision of being the most customer-centric car dealership group in the USA couldn't stay at the company. Asbury even made every employee sign "contracts" that they would put customer satisfaction first going forward. Employees, including some high-performing sellers, who weren't on board left the company, or were asked to leave. There were no exceptions.

- **Train employees:** Asbury made all employees take courses on customer centricity. These courses focused on practical examples of great customer experiences and role-play exercises.

- **Hire more scientifically:** Asbury revamped its hiring process to align new hires with its culture of customer satisfaction and ensure they had the right traits to succeed. They used the Caliper system to predict candidate success through personality profiles, while a new VP of psychology designed complementary interviews. A hiring committee vetted all candidates, ensuring thorough and culture-focused hiring decisions.

- **Share information broadly:** Asbury built a simple tool to spot important CX trends across all its Google reviews and made those available to all employees. Asbury has found that three- and four-star reviews are the most insightful, and Asbury encourages employees to read them all.

- **Align incentives:** These reviews are also key to an employee's success at Asbury. In fact, a salesperson at Asbury can't receive internet leads if their customer service score is not perfect, even if they close a high percentage of these leads.

- **Solicit employee ideas:** Asbury developed a simple system to empower every employee to generate CX improvement ideas. This wasn't just lip service. These ideas were taken seriously, and each was considered.

- **Standardize and scale:** To speed up the implementation of solutions, Asbury developed a standardized process to roll out new ideas: They work with one or two of the dealers to test a new solution, prove the economic value for the dealer, then scale the solution to all dealers very quickly.

7

IMPROVE FASTER
THAN COMPETITORS

S equoias adapt remarkably well. They have even evolved to withstand Northern California's frequent wildfires, with their bark containing tannic acid, the same chemical in fire extinguishers, that makes them almost fireproof. And their cones have adapted to release seeds more effectively when exposed to the heat from fires.

Similarly, corporate sequoias improve faster than competitors. For instance, a study found that top-performing companies were able to make changes of average complexity, such as adding a product feature or updating pricing logic, within two to four months compared to average companies that took up to a year. The result for the faster companies? Up to 35 percent higher revenue growth and 10 percent greater profit margins.[1]

Top companies move faster because they've developed a finely tuned system to rapidly generate, test, and implement new ideas. They also continuously focus on improving this system, ensuring it becomes faster and more effective over time. I call this approach of improving the process "getting better at getting better."

The ability to get better at getting better is often the most sustainable competitive advantage for an organization, much like it is for living organisms. Darwin's concept of survival of the fittest is frequently misunderstood—it's not about being the strongest but about being the one that adapts the fastest. Jeff Bezos captured this concept succinctly: "Our success at Amazon is directly tied to how many experiments we run—per year, per month, per week, per day."[2]

A very successful entrepreneur explained this idea with a chess analogy during a recent conversation: "If I played chess against a grandmaster, I'd lose every game. But if I got two moves for every one they made, I'd win every time. My success isn't because I'm the smartest, the most aggressive, or the most creative. I just make more moves."

Neil Hoyne from Google shared an amazing story. In a meeting with one of the world's best companies, he proposed a new concept. To his surprise, a few attendees opened their laptops and appeared to tune out. Concerned that he had lost their interest, Neil continued with his presentation, feeling uneasy. At the end of the hour-long meeting, he asked if the group was willing to test the concept. One of the seemingly disengaged participants responded, "The test is already done. It worked. Thank you for the suggestion."

But as Jasper Malcolmson, head of growth at Gusto and previously at Robinhood and Opendoor, reminds us, testing itself isn't the goal—results are: "In the end, what matters is outcomes, not the number of tests. The top companies use testing as one of the tools to drive meaningful business results, not as an end in itself."

While I agree with Jasper that the quantity of tests isn't the most critical metric, doing more tests often leads to better results. It also helps create a more dynamic culture focused on continuous improvement. Running more tests also means achieving a meaningful number of wins, helping to balance out the financial and emotional costs of failures. In contrast, a company that conducts only a handful of tests each year might experience only failure, making each failure feel far more consequential.

In earlier chapters, I shared six transformative strategies to help your company grow into a towering sequoia. But there are countless other ideas worth exploring. The speed at which you can test and deploy these ideas will likely determine how long you stay a sequoia.

INTERNET COMPANY INCREASES
TESTING BY TWENTY-FIVE TIMES IN ONE YEAR

In 2024, I met the CEO of an internet company who was frustrated with his company's lack of testing. The company was doing only about a hundred relatively small tests a month, a surprisingly low number given their size and aspirations. The CEO was determined to increase the number and the business impact of these tests.

At the time, testing was scattered across the organization, with no clear ownership. To address this issue, the CEO centralized testing into a dedicated growth team, which quickly began generating, prioritizing, testing, and scaling new ideas.

But testing was difficult and slow. After the team implemented a thorough posttest review that included analyzing the issues that slowed testing down, they discovered that a significant number of tests required legal approval. To address this bottleneck, they added a part-time attorney to the growth team. Similarly, they realized that many tests were delayed because they relied on a slow-moving external creative agency. In response, they hired an in-house designer.

The team continued identifying and resolving obstacles as they arose. They introduced automation tools, streamlined data collection, and standardized reporting.

After a few months, the team's testing velocity increased by ten times, and they faced an unexpected challenge: They started running out of good ideas to test. To address this issue, they proposed a company-wide monthly contest to crowdsource testing ideas. All employees were encouraged to submit ideas, explaining how their proposed test would improve business results and delight customers, ideally high-CLV customers, though that wasn't explicitly stated.

The CEO enthusiastically supported the initiative and personally announced the winners at the monthly all-hands meetings. The winners received significant monetary rewards and generous praise for their outstanding ideas. Notably, the awards were granted based on the quality of the idea itself, not on whether the hypothesis was ultimately proven right or wrong. This is a practice embraced by X (The Moonshot Factory), Google's innovation lab dedicated to creating breakthrough technologies. As its leader, Astro Teller, explains, "If you give out the award before you've run the experiment, people begin to genuinely feel that you care about the quality of the question [they're asking]."[3]

The combination of a centralized team, continuous improvement of the testing process, and company-wide engagement turned what was once a slow and scattered effort into a high-velocity, high-impact growth engine. After less than a year, the team was executing more than twenty-five hundred tests a month, a twenty-five times improvement. The impact on business results and customer satisfaction was substantial.

WHY DO SO FEW COMPANIES IMPROVE THIS QUICKLY?

You'd think every company would embrace the idea of getting better at getting better. But in my meetings with senior executives, I found that many were unwilling to test new ideas. From my experience, this resistance happens for a few key reasons.

Legacy Thinking

Some companies are so rooted in their traditional ways that they resist even the most compelling evidence for change. In 2024, I proposed a plan to rapidly improve the website and digital marketing efforts of a retailer with below average e-commerce results. The CEO's response? "Our main strategy isn't about e-commerce or paid advertising. We put our stores near highways, and customers drop in because they see our stores from the highway."

I shared data showing that most customers, especially customers with high disposable income, research online before deciding to drive to a store, making the case that a great e-commerce strategy was important to drive store sales. The CEO's response? "Our customers just aren't like everyone else and are less interested in researching online."

After an hour of back-and-forth that went nowhere, I felt I had no choice but to try to shock the company into action. So I asked, "If your customers visit stores only because they see you from the highway, and they're not influenced by paid advertising, why are you still spending tens of millions of dollars a year on paper flyers?"

Culture of Debate Instead of Action

Imagine you're a movie executive and discover a magical AI advertising tool that will show your movie trailer to tens of millions of moviegoers. Around five million of them will then head to a theater showing your film, at a cost of just $0.50 per visit. If it works, this strategy will generate $27.5 million in cash flow for your next movie.[4]

Or imagine you're a hotel executive and learn that you can drive around two million potential guests to visit your hotel in person, at a cost of just $5 per walk-in. If it works, this strategy could unlock significant profitable growth for your business.

In meetings with companies across various industries, I proposed this very strategy, called Local Campaigns, and saw two distinct reactions.

Some organizations embraced the idea and moved quickly to test it, calling it a "no-brainer."

Others spent most of the meeting debating, asking questions like: "How do you track the people who visit our hotels? Is it at least 90 percent accurate?" "Can you prove that people who saw the ads and showed up to the hotel actually booked a room?" "How do we know what type of room they'll book, how long they'll stay, and how to calculate the ROAS?"

Thankfully, most of the time, a senior executive would intervene, saying something like, "If we make $250 in profit per average hotel stay, less than 2 percent of these walk-in customers would need to book a room to make this investment worthwhile. Let's test this idea."

But more often than you can imagine, some companies would refuse to even test this remarkable tool. In my experience, companies like that are very unlikely to become sequoias until they change their culture.

Already-Tried-It Syndrome

Just because an idea failed in the past doesn't mean it won't work today. Market dynamics, customer behaviors, and technologies evolve. Many ideas also previously fail not because they are flawed but because of poor execution, lack of resources, or timing. Revisiting these ideas with fresh perspectives, modern tools, and a clearer understanding of what has changed can lead to breakthroughs.

For example, QR codes were once considered a failed experiment but have seen a resurgence due to changing customer behaviors and technology.

Seth van der Swaagh from Google shares another insightful story: "Google offers a tool called Broad Match that allows a company's ads to appear for a lot more customer searches. In the past, these ads were not always well targeted, and some advertisers experienced poor results. But the tool has since been significantly improved and is now essential for scaling a Google Ads campaign. A mortgage provider recently implemented it and, despite operating in a challenging mortgage environment, achieved their first revenue and profit growth in years. Unfortunately, many seasoned digital marketers refuse to give Broad Match another chance, clinging to outdated perceptions of its performance, to their detriment."

Overconfidence

Recently, I met with executives of a car company who confidently declared they were on the verge of catching Tesla in the EV market. I asked them, "If the race for electric vehicle dominance were a hundred-meter sprint, where would you place yourself and Tesla right now?" They replied, "Tesla is at the fifty-meter mark, and we're at thirty meters." My follow-up question, meant to help the company become more realistic and move faster, provoked a strong reaction: "Who's running faster?"

Such overconfidence can be dangerous. By underestimating competitors and overestimating their own capabilities, companies can fail to encourage their teams to take more risks and test newer things.

Feeling Overwhelmed

Many executives feel overwhelmed by the idea of starting and scaling an improvement system because it can seem like a big departure from how the company currently operates. It's important to remember that even the best in the world developed their skills gradually. For instance, Amazon and Booking.com, two of the top testing organizations in the world, took more than seven years to implement a structured testing program. Amazon started controlled experiments in 2002 and scaled dramatically, growing from 546 tests to 12,000 annually by 2011 when it built its Weblab testing platform.[5]

A FIVE-STEP PROCESS TO GET BETTER AT GETTING BETTER

Many companies get better at getting better. For example, a beverage company successfully reduced its product development cycle from one year to just one month by testing new generative AI technologies.[6] To begin, they used a large language model tool and social media monitoring software to analyze vast amounts of nonconfidential customer data, gaining insights into flavor preferences in just one day, a process that typically would have taken months of traditional market research.

During the design phase, the company used a text-to-image generative AI tool to produce thirty high-quality beverage concepts in a single day. These concepts were quickly tested with consumers in the field, helping the marketing team quickly narrow the options to three promising candidates. The flavor team then developed multiple variations of each candidate and conducted two weeks of taste tests to identify the winning formula. Simultaneously, the marketing team tested hundreds of AI-generated packaging designs, completing this process within the same two-week period.

Enterprise Rent-A-Car has created one of the best systems to get better at getting better, despite facing a unique challenge due to its franchise model, where many of its ninety-five hundred branches in a hundred countries operate semi-independently. The fantastic book *The Ultimate Question 2.0* details Enterprise's great process for getting better at getting better.[7]

Enterprise gathers a modified NPS score for many of its rentals by sending postrental surveys to customers. Unlike anonymous feedback, the NPS score is tied directly to each customer's rental record, giving Enterprise detailed insights into the NPS scores of individual customers, not just aggregated scores.

This single piece of data becomes a gold mine of insights, as it allows Enterprise to analyze near–real time changes in customer satisfaction by customer segment (for example, it might include high-CLV customers, business travelers, first-time renters), by branch, and even by individual employees responsible for the rental.

This data is shared with each branch that uses it to make rapid corrections. Branch employees are also encouraged to try new ideas to increase the branch's NPS score. For example, Enterprise's "We'll pick you up" strategy was not a corporate initiative but was invented by a branch manager in Orlando.

A central team also monitors this data from headquarters in St. Louis. When the team detects a significant change in a branch's score, they act quickly. They analyze customer feedback, conduct interviews with branch managers and employees, and scour operational data with the goal of finding great ideas other branches can emulate.

When the central team identifies a promising new idea, they work with a small subset of other branches who volunteer to test the idea. These tests are measured rigorously against NPS data and other key performance indicators, including financial data.

Once a test shows an idea works, it's rolled out more broadly. But branches are never forced to adopt an idea, so they can maintain their independence and flexibility. At the same time, branches are highly motivated to increase NPS through rewards and recognition programs, which celebrate top performers. There is also an accountability element: Only managers whose branches have a high NPS can get a senior job at headquarters.

What an extraordinary system. It seamlessly blends the strengths of bottom-up innovation with top-down best practice sharing. Best of all, participation is entirely voluntary, ensuring that franchisees feel empowered rather than coerced into adopting ideas they don't genuinely believe in.

Rick Shadyac of ALSAC/St. Jude offers this advice, reinforcing the theme of "opening the aperture" mentioned in chapter 5: "One of the most important ways to improve faster and tackle complex digital transformations is to open the aperture. For example, I often remind my team that our biggest competitor isn't other nonprofits—it's Facebook and others, which are increasingly becoming key intermediaries between donors and nonprofits. To remain successful, we must be as good as Facebook. That's why one of our top priorities today is AI."

Below is a low-risk and cost-effective five-step process to help your company quickly get better at getting better.

STEP 1—CREATE A CENTRALIZED
GROWTH TEAM SET UP FOR SUCCESS

Many companies that excel at getting better at getting better have a centralized growth team, separate from the centralized CX team we covered in chapter 6. Having a central growth team doesn't preclude the creation of other growth teams inside individual divisions or departments. The central growth team's role is to focus on the broader customer journey, ensuring a holistic view and optimizing the overall experience across the organization, while other growth teams have a narrower scope.

The marketing department is an ideal place to start your first growth team because marketing tests are generally easier to run and measure than other types of tests. Starting a growth team in marketing is fairly simple, inexpensive, and can deliver quick results.

I recommend the team report directly to the CMO and at first focus only on improving marketing results. Over time, the team's scope should expand beyond marketing. Depending on the company's needs, the team can continue reporting to the CMO or transition to the COO, the CEO, or a dedicated chief growth officer.

To quickly build an effective marketing growth team:

Start Small

A new marketing growth team should be small, nimble, and cross-functional. We recommend at least a data scientist with a lot of testing experience, a performance marketer with deep understanding of the Google and Facebook advertising systems, an email marketer, and a web/app developer familiar with the latest design tools. Over time, as the team focuses on more complex issues, it will likely need to add more people with complementary skills.

One way to start the team quickly and inexpensively is to look for part-time volunteers for a few short projects to get some quick wins to make the case for funding a full-time team.

Luc Levesque, formerly chief growth officer at Shopify, has a lot of experience building successful growth teams: "You want people who've done it before, ideally at smaller companies. They need to demonstrate they had a lot of impact on a previous growth team and have a strong bias for action. You're not looking for intellectuals; you're looking for people who get a huge kick out of improving a key metric every day."

Give the Team the Right Tools

Equip the team with tools that enable them to work independently, without the help of the IT team, ensuring they can remain agile and avoid delays. The tools needed are different for every company and will change over time. Start with the bare minimum and add more over time. Tools to consider include:

- A/B and multivariate testing tools like Optimizely or Visual Website Optimizer
- robust analytics tools like Google Analytics 4, Amplitude, or Mixpanel
- email marketing and automation platforms like HubSpot, Marketo, or Klaviyo

- SEO and content tools like Ahrefs, SEMrush, or Moz

- landing page solutions like Unbounce, Instapage, or Leadpages

- AI tools like Figma AI, Zapier or Make.com, Jasper.ai or ChatGPT, Canva or Adcreative.ai, Albert.ai or Pattern89, and Runway ML or Sora[8]

- as the team gets bigger and does more complex tests, it may make sense to implement tools like a CDP to unify customer data across multiple sources; a personalization engine to deliver tailored experiences at scale based on user behavior and preferences; propensity modeling tools to help build forecast models; data visualization software to help the team effectively interpret and present complex test results; and cloud data warehousing solutions to manage large datasets and enable efficient querying for test analysis.

Establish Clear Guidelines from the Beginning

Successful growth teams move fast. An important reason for their speed is a well-defined framework for what they can test, how to test, and how to evaluate results. With clear rules in place, they can implement successful ideas without needing constant approval while minimizing risks. Key components of testing guidelines should include:

- **Data restrictions and other ethical considerations:** Protecting customer privacy is critical. Define what existing customer data the team can access and what new data they are allowed to collect. Also clearly define other ethical considerations such as avoiding deceptive practices, ensuring fairness for all customers, and being transparent.

- **Experimentation boundaries:** Determine where tests can be conducted. Common approaches include geofencing (for example, running tests only in a small region), limiting the scope to small populations (for example, allowing experiments as long as they impact no more than 1 percent of users), and limiting the types of tests (for example, pricing tests may require approval from the CFO).

- **Guardrails for risks:** Define clear limits for acceptable risks to prevent negative outcomes (for example, tests should not cause a drop of more than a certain percentage in daily profits or customer satisfaction or an increase of a certain percentage in page load speed). If any of these thresholds are hit, the test is paused, and the results are analyzed to mitigate further risks.

STEP 2—SET UP THE RIGHT METRICS

To establish from the outset that the central growth team is, as Jasper Malcolmson calls it, "an outcome team, not a testing team," begin with well-defined projects tied to clear business metrics and time frames (for example, reduce churn of this high-CLV segment by 15 percent in three months). Continue with this project-driven approach until the team consistently achieves its objectives.

Then introduce simple KPIs that give the team a clear direction and more autonomy to prioritize projects on their own. These metrics may not be perfect, but they are easy to track and are good metrics for testing quickly. Ideally the KPI should be a leading, not a lagging, indicator. For example:

- Airbnb measures nights booked.[9]
- Spotify focuses on listen time.[10]
- YouTube uses watch time.[11]
- Progressive monitors the number of products per household.[12]

- Quora tracks questions answered.[13]
- SpaceX tracks cost per kilogram of payload launched.[14]

Improving the KPI should clearly improve the company's economics and ideally create a competitive advantage that's difficult for others to replicate. SpaceX revolutionized the orbital launch industry by eliminating cost-plus billing and instead charging a fixed fee to launch payloads into orbit. This pricing model incentivized SpaceX to reduce launch costs, unlike competitors who profited more as costs increased.

Over time, SpaceX cut orbital launch costs from $12,000 per kilogram to $2,000 per kilogram.[15] Their launch fees are now about half of Boeing's, at $67 million[16] compared to $118 million.[17] This cost efficiency enabled SpaceX to dominate the market, launching roughly 80 percent of the world's orbital payloads in 2023.[18]

As SpaceX further reduces its launch costs—Starship is projected to bring costs down to $200 per kilogram[19]—it is likely to widen its lead over competitors even more. For SpaceX, the cost-per-kilogram-of-payload metric is not just a useful KPI; it is a strategic priority that drives its ability to outpace rivals and maintain dominance in the industry.

Luc Levesque, who has guided many growth teams in selecting KPIs, stresses the importance of focus: "A growth team needs incredible focus on one North Star metric. That doesn't mean ignoring other metrics that track the health of the business. It means their optimization efforts revolve around one key metric. The North Star metric should be a powerful lever that can drive significant business results. Even if it's not perfect, pick the best metric available."

Luc also highlights the need for both consistency and flexibility: "The North Star metric should remain consistent over time to ensure focus, but it's equally important to revisit it periodically. As the metric becomes harder to improve or starts to limit creative thinking, introducing a new metric can spark fresh innovation and progress."

Over time, some growth teams start using more sophisticated metrics similar to the ones in figure 7.1 for a fictitious streaming company:

FIGURE 7.1 GROWTH TEAM DASHBOARD EXAMPLE

Test #	Description	Start	End	CLV Impact	NPS Impact	Main Blocker
1032	20% off subscription for 2-year renewal to 10,000 test group renewing next month	12/1/24	1/13/25	$5M	+5	Testing pricing requires 4 approvals
1032	Recommend children content in adult feed to 5,000 test group not watching children's content	12/1/24	1/14/25	-$1M	-5	Changing recommendation engine takes 12 hrs
1034	Increase price by 20% for UltraHD watch experience to 1,000 test group	12/2/24	1/16/25	$3M	-10	Testing new price tiers requires 4 approvals
...	...	...	...	...	...	...
1435	Test new landing page with highest rated shows personalized for each customer to 500 test group	12/4/24	1/20/25	$1M	+10	Much easier to change recommendation engine, takes 1 hr
		Total for Jan 2025		$62M 97% of goal +25% YoY	+5	

The Change in CLV for Each Test

The previously shown dashboard measures financial outcomes by tracking the change in CLV for every test. It does so by comparing CLV before and after the test for both a control and test group, as discussed in chapter 4. The change in CLV is the best metric to measure the results of many tests because it:

- focuses on longer-term profits, the financial metric a sequoia should care about the most;

- avoids many of the measurement challenges typical in digital advertising testing since it relies on CRM data, not advertising attribution models;

- ensures a holistic view of the test's impact across the customer journey since the change in CLV is a more comprehensive metric than metrics that look only at a slice of a customer's behavior, like average order value or churn; and

- ensures an apples-to-apples comparison for all kinds of tests, whether it's a new product launch, a pricing change, a new recommendation engine, or a personalized offer.

Total CLV Increase

To motivate the growth team to prioritize the ideas with the biggest impact and increase velocity, this dashboard tracks the total CLV increase generated by the team each month, comparing it to the same period last year and against a monthly goal. The total CLV increase is calculated by summing up the change in CLV from all tests conducted.

The Change in NPS from Each Test

To ensure that tests don't increase CLV at the expense of customer satisfaction, this dashboard tracks the change in NPS for each test. This is the guardrail metric. This company is fortunate to have customer-level

NPS data, similar to Enterprise, allowing it to easily measure the change in NPS for the test and control groups before and after a test.

Most companies, however, lack customer satisfaction data at the individual customer level. An effective alternative is to conduct a regional test and evaluate changes in customer satisfaction within that region before and after the experiment. This can be achieved using regional NPS data, publicly accessible sources such as Yelp reviews, or insights from social media listening. Although this approach doesn't offer the precision of a true A/B test, it provides a practical way to mitigate potential negative impacts on customer satisfaction resulting from the test.

The Main Blocker

To continue to accelerate the velocity of testing, the team documents any obstacles encountered during the testing process. By identifying recurring issues, the team can proactively address them and streamline future testing efforts.

STEP 3—FIND AND PRIORITIZE THE BEST IDEAS

Getting better at getting better begins with great ideas tailored to specific customer segments. For example, ideas to increase the CLV of young customers may differ significantly from those aimed at older customers. As mentioned previously, it's important to pay particular attention to ideas that can increase the CLV of already-good customers. The following are strategies for sourcing ideas.

Growth Team Ideas

At companies with dedicated growth teams, the growth team is often the primary source of new ideas. These teams typically consist of members with diverse backgrounds and experience from other organizations, bringing with them a playbook of proven strategies for improving CLV.

To help the growth team generate high-quality ideas, it is essential to provide them with rigorous training. This training should focus on the company's business economics, key growth drivers, and an in-depth understanding of its high-CLV customer segments.

Historical Successes

An effective method for finding ideas is to spread to more customers what has already worked for a subset of customers. You can identify the customers whose CLV has increased the most recently (those in the right-most third of the chart in figure 4.2), and reverse engineer the actions taken during that period to drive these improvements. These insights can then be tested on other customer segments to evaluate their broader applicability and effectiveness.

Customer Research

Customer research can be a rich source of great ideas. As highlighted in chapter 6, conducting in-depth research into the preferences, pain points, and behaviors of high-CLV customer segments can spark innovative ideas. One particularly effective approach I've seen is interviewing customers who have experienced the largest increase in CLV over the past few months to uncover the factors driving that increase.

Online Monitoring

Real-time customer feedback monitoring can be a gold mine for innovation. For example, Dior uses Astra, an advanced AI platform designed to aggregate customer feedback from diverse channels, including Google reviews, product pages, customer service interactions, satisfaction surveys, live shopping sessions, and more. By synthesizing all this data, Astra provides real-time insights into emerging trends, potential issues, and shifts in consumer sentiment.[20]

Employee Ideas

Some of the best ideas can come from employees. For example, the idea for Prime originated from an engineer's suggestion in Amazon's employee feedback program. To create a world-class employee ideas program, follow the example of the internet company that increased tests by twenty-five times described previously.

Competitive Analysis

Competitor analysis is a powerful tool for generating new ideas, especially when you look beyond your geography and industry. Estelle Metayer, founder of Competia, has more than thirty years of experience advising CEOs on competitive intelligence. Here are her top competitive analysis strategies:

- **Understand customer journeys:** Use tools like Google Analytics to analyze the websites customers visit before and after yours to identify the options they are considering. Enrich this data with tools like VisitorQueue and session replay technologies to map user journeys and pinpoint friction points in your CX.

- **Analyze competitors' strategy:** Tools like Meltwater or Semrush can reveal how customers engage with competitor sites. Downloading main competitors' entire websites and using AI to spot changes shows the evolution of their digital CX, suggesting new ideas to test.

- **Track sentiment about competitors:** Tools such as SocialMention, Radian6, or Sysomos track customer sentiment over time, exposing vulnerabilities in competitors' offerings and generating improvement ideas for your own business.

- **Leverage alternative data:** Sources like satellite imagery, credit card transactions, and mobile location data can provide unique insights into consumer behavior, spending patterns, and preferences that generate new ideas.

Partner Suggestions

Neil Hoyne tells the story of a meeting with a company he considers one of the best in the world at sourcing and testing new ideas. Their request was simple yet powerful: "Tell us what we're not doing but should be. No matter how crazy the idea sounds, or even if it's failed multiple times, we want to hear it because we want to learn from all the work you're doing with your smartest customers." This company was so good at testing that their odds of success were much higher than others, so they wanted to hear all the ideas.

With these systems in place, your growth team should have a constant stream of great ideas. The next crucial step is prioritization. Here's a way to do it well.

Eliminate the Majority of Ideas

It's important to pursue only the ideas that make sense. At Robinhood and Opendoor, Jasper Malcolmson personally reviewed all major ideas to ensure they were worth pursuing. Given the complexity of their business models and economics, he confirmed that each idea would affect the right metric enough to justify the effort involved: "We eliminated at least 60 percent of the proposed tests this way, saving ourselves a tremendous amount of time and resources." Luc Levesque shares a similar approach: "At Shopify, we said no to absolutely everything that did not contribute to growing our North Star metric. In fact, I even gave back a team of three hundred people to another Shopify executive because the team could not help improve our North Star metric."

It's also critical to eliminate ideas that, even if successfully tested, are unlikely to be implemented. I've worked with some retailers who tested the same idea multiple times over many years. The tests consistently showed that many customers who search online purchase in-store. The goal of these tests was to justify sharing store sales data with Google so Google Ads could increase omnichannel profits. Despite the proven potential of this strategy, as demonstrated earlier with Pandora, and almost all tests yielding positive results, many of these retailers never shared their store sales data with Google. So why test it in the first place?

Testing ideas that won't be implemented, even after a successful test, is not only a waste of time and resources but also deeply demoralizing for the growth team. In my experience, it often leads to the loss of superstar members of the team.

To ensure that successful tests are implemented, some growth teams prioritize ideas they can implement independently, without relying on other teams. For ideas that require collaboration with other teams, they secure precommitments, often in writing, from all necessary stakeholders to ensure the idea will be implemented before investing any time testing it.

Start with Ideas That Don't Need Testing

Many growth teams have been trained to test all ideas as scientifically as possible. But this approach isn't always necessary. For easy-to-deploy ideas with a high likelihood of success, the best approach is often to simply launch the ideas and monitor progress.

Luc Levesque calls these YOLO (you only live once) ideas. He emphasizes that life is short, and there's no time to waste. Speed should take precedence over perfection. Luc often challenges his growth teams by asking, "Can we YOLO this idea instead of testing it?"

Jasper Malcolmson shares a similar philosophy: "Growth teams should focus on developing a deep understanding of customers and business economics. With this knowledge, they can rely on sound judgment to move faster, rather than testing everything."

Prioritize the Rest Effectively

Most growth teams use a systematic, points-based approach, such as the ICE (impact, confidence, effort) scoring model, to prioritize tests. They prioritize ideas that have the potential to increase CLV the most while also increasing NPS, that can be tested rapidly with minimal investment, ensuring momentum stays high, and that can be rolled out quickly and inexpensively after testing. Early on in a new testing program, the bias should be for quick wins, even if the impact is not the highest. As the team gains more credibility, it should prioritize more complex ideas with the potential for more impact.

STEP 4—RADICALLY IMPROVE TESTING CAPABILITIES

Once the team has prioritized the list of ideas that should be tested, it's time to optimize the testing process. Here are proven principles to help a growth team test better and faster.[21]

Start with a Clear Hypothesis

Every test should begin with a measurable hypothesis. For example, "Sending this offer will increase CLV by 1 percent while not decreasing NPS." This provides clarity, focuses the team on specific outcomes, and ensures everyone aligns on what success looks like.

Specify the Level of Confidence Required

Testing is not about getting perfect answers but about making better-informed decisions. Since there is often a trade-off between the effort required to conduct a test and the level of confidence it provides, teams must decide, up front, whether additional confidence is worth the investment. For example, if increasing the level of confidence from 70 to 80 percent requires an extra three months of testing, is it worth it?

The level of confidence for what Jeff Bezos calls type 1 decisions—those with large, hard-to-reverse impacts like launching Amazon Prime, starting a new product category, or significantly changing pricing strategy—should be high. For type 2 decisions, which are easier to reverse, like modifying website copy or sending an offer to a small subset of customers—they should be much lower.

Set a Specific Time Frame

Every test should have a clear, predetermined time frame to prevent over-analysis and ensure progress. Duration depends on the scope of the idea. For smaller ideas, teams should test quickly, get the minimum information they need to make a better decision, and move on.

For more transformational ideas, teams should allow for a much longer time frame and multiple iterations if necessary because transformational ideas often require many attempts to refine and implement successfully.

GiveDirectly knew that donors who choose monthly donations have a CLV that's twelve times higher on average. To increase the percentage of donors who donate monthly, GiveDirectly asked donors who were giving a onetime donation (for example, a onetime $25 donation) to switch to a monthly donation (for example, $5 per month). While this increased the likelihood that donors would donate monthly by 700 percent, it decreased total donors by 10 percent by adding an extra step in the donation process, increasing friction. The increase in monthly donations wasn't enough to compensate for the decrease in donors so the test was not successful. Instead of giving up, GiveDirectly tried a new approach. They removed the extra step and simply defaulted to monthly donations on their main giving page, which increased donations significantly.[22]

Standardize the Testing Process

Enterprise and Asbury have standardized their testing. They pilot new ideas in select volunteer locations and carefully measure the impact of each idea on NPS and financial metrics. They also both actively seek input from frontline employees at the pilot locations to gain valuable insights about how the idea is working in practice. Based on the feedback and results, they refine the idea before a wider rollout.

Some companies standardize other parts of the testing process. They use consistent hypothesis frameworks, uniform test summary reports, clear data standards, and standardized communication protocols to ensure cross-functional alignment and transparent reporting to senior leadership. They also create a learning repository, a centralized database of test results and insights, which helps avoid repeating failed experiments and accelerates knowledge-sharing across teams.

The best testing systems are also flexible enough so that growth teams can follow a nonstandard process when it makes sense.

Design the Best Minimum Viable Test (MVT)

An MVT is the simplest possible test that gives a growth team the confidence level it needs to accept or reject a hypothesis while of course complying with any laws and internal governance rules. For some tests, like testing a new drug, MVT needs to be very scientific, but for others they can be as simple as an A/B test that lasts an hour. By focusing on MVTs, teams can radically increase the velocity of testing while getting just enough information to make informed decisions.

I'm not sure how Asbury tested their app that allows customers to view videos of proposed repairs and approve them, but here's one approach they could have taken using an MVT. They could start by training a single mechanic to use a smartphone to record brief videos explaining the proposed repairs. These videos could then be emailed directly to customers. This low-cost, manual method would prioritize testing the core concept: whether customers are more likely to trust repair estimates when they are accompanied by a video explanation.

Only after validating the idea, proving that videos increase customer trust and engagement, should the company invest in building a dedicated app to automate the process, train all mechanics, and roll it out to every customer. This incremental approach minimizes risk and ensures resources are focused on a proven solution.

Using its Design for Delight methodology, Intuit tests new features through manual prototypes in real customer environments. For instance, guided tax preparation might initially be tested by using live customer support representatives before automating the process in software.[23]

Instead of immediately building their platform, Dropbox created a short explainer video demonstrating the product's functionality. The video generated significant interest, helping validate the concept without heavy development costs.[24]

Instead of building an MVT, Jasper Malcolmson's team at Opendoor went all in on generative AI: "Our team got really excited about gen AI, and we spent nine months building an advanced AI chatbot to talk to prospective customers through SMS only to find that any type of interaction, like a simple email, had the same impact. In hindsight, we should have tested the chatbot idea by manually typing responses in a fake chatbot and comparing that to email before investing a ton of time deploying the technology."

GiveDirectly made the same mistake. Drawing on evidence from other nonprofits suggesting that matching donors with individual recipients could significantly boost CLV, GiveDirectly created a system where donors received quarterly emails featuring photos and stories about the progress of their recipient. But GiveDirectly's recipient-matching feature, which was complex and costly to create in the first place, also encountered significant operational hurdles, including the need for field teams to collect recipient stories by traveling to remote villages, which was logistically challenging and costly. Additionally, the product team spent more than twenty hours each month on manual quality assurance tasks, such as troubleshooting delays, ensuring accurate updates, and rematching donors when recipients relocated. The customer service team also faced a high volume of donor inquiries about delayed updates. Despite these extensive efforts, the feature did not improve CLV at all.[25]

Undeterred, GiveDirectly tested a much simpler concept, which is what they should have done in the first place. Instead of linking a donor with an individual recipient, they linked them to a specific village. To test this approach, they sent emails specifying that donations supported a specific village in Rwanda compared to emails stating donations went to Rwanda in general. The village-specific emails performed 58 percent better than the generic ones. GiveDirectly rolled out this new system of matching donors with the results of a specific village.

Test with High-CLV Audiences

As described previously, it's important to test ideas on high-CLV audiences because these audiences might want something completely different from the average customer. To run tests for current high-CLV customers, you can simply use email to target only a test and control group of high-CLV customers. If you want to use paid media, you can upload your top 20 percent CLV customers into Google's Customer Match and Similar Audiences, or Facebook's Lookalike audiences and test landing pages for this audience.

Use AI to Test Faster and Smarter

Leveraging AI, when it makes sense, can significantly speed up testing. Here are a few examples:

- **Generate content at scale:** AI can generate nearly infinite product/service descriptions, emails, offers, website content, and ads, basically for free. In the AI marketing class I teach, we even have a section, led by Rory Flynn, where he demonstrates how to generate a thousand unique banner and video ads in just an hour.

- **Prototype websites and apps in hours:** With AI-powered design platforms like Figma AI, companies can create website or app prototypes in hours, not weeks. These tools can rapidly transform sketches, wireframes, or even text prompts into fully interactive designs, enabling teams to test new user interfaces and features with minimal up-front investment.

  Once the prototypes are ready, they can be quickly tested using platforms like UserTesting or Alida, which gather real-time feedback from target users through recorded sessions that highlight usability issues and preferences, or Maze, a rapid user-testing platform that integrates directly with Figma, allowing for usability tests, surveys, and heatmaps.

- **Get AI to test for you.** AI tools like Keak can do website testing automatically for you. The tool generates hypotheses on its own, then tests and deploys them. Other tools like Offerfit can A/B test different personalized emails with different offers to customers. Brinks Home, Brinks's home security division, says it has increased the number of tests it does from a few to fifty thousand a day.[26]

Remove Barriers to Testing

As mentioned earlier, an important aspect of improving testing is to identify and address the primary bottlenecks in the process. One effective approach is conducting rigorous posttest analyses, where teams evaluate not only the outcomes but also opportunities to accelerate testing. Over time, these reviews will uncover specific obstacles that are slowing down the testing process.

Set Up a Test Follow-Up Process

Jasper Malcomson makes an important point: "Teams like to be able to run experiments and get results quickly. While this helps increase testing velocity, which is critical, it may lead to missing the longer-term impact of tests. For example, introducing an educational step in an onboarding journey might introduce some friction and lower short-term results but could significantly increase CLV over the long term."

Luc Levesque and Jasper offer the same advice: Revisit all major tests after a few months to ensure the results still hold, and make adjustments if they don't. For example, Shopify reviews the outcome of all major tests over a two-year period, which frequently leads to revised conclusions.[27]

STEP 5—IMPLEMENT SOLUTIONS QUICKLY

Successful tests are great, but increasing CLV and NPS is better. We've worked with many growth teams that ran a lot of successful tests but struggled to get their ideas implemented. This not only halts progress but demoralizes the team. To implement more solutions more rapidly:

Focus on Tests the Growth Team Can Implement Itself

As noted earlier, the best way to ensure tests are implemented is to focus, at least initially, on tests the growth team can implement by itself. For solutions requiring external help to scale, secure written precommitments to implement the solution before running the tests.

Set Up Clear Implementation Decision Rules

Developing clear implementation decision rules is essential to avoid delays and empower the growth team to act. For example, could a growth team implement a test that increased CLV by 3 percent but decreased NPS by 2 points? If the growth team needs to seek approval from multiple stakeholders every time it wants to implement a test, long delays are inevitable, and the team's impact and morale will suffer.

Implement a Minimum Viable Solution (MVS)

An MVS is the simplest possible solution that delivers a large portion of the desired benefits with minimal effort, cost, and complexity. Deploying an MVS allows organizations to validate their test results in a real-world context, learn from the deployment, and gather additional feedback before implementing a more robust solution. It reduces time-to-value and avoids the trap of overengineering a solution before its core elements have been validated at scale.

A retailer struggling to show product availability online could offer real-time stock updates for very high-demand products in flagship stores. To accomplish this, they would need to improve product availability data for a few hundred products, not the hundreds of thousands of products available in all stores.

Airbnb rolled out the addition of Experiences, a platform for booking activities hosted by locals, by initially offering a limited selection in specific cities. Instead of a broad, complex rollout, Airbnb focused on a manageable number of experiences to gather user feedback and understand demand. The MVT approach allowed Airbnb to refine the feature based on real user interactions before expanding globally.[28]

I recently worked with a company that had proven with a simple test that sending personalized email offers to high-CLV customers significantly increased CLV. Instead of deploying a full-fledged and expensive AI tool to personalize every email based on a complex next-best-action model, they manually segmented customers and personalized offers for each segment. This solution was deployed in a week and increased CLV by 7 percent. A year later, when the full AI system was in place, it increased CLV by 9 percent. By implementing an MVS first, this company achieved nearly 80 percent of the benefit in 2 percent of the time and at a very low cost. Of course, if the full solution is relatively simple and inexpensive to implement, it may make sense to skip the MVS and deploy the full system right away.

Standardize the Implementation Process

Many successful companies have developed highly standardized systems for implementing successful ideas, ensuring efficient scaling and adoption across their organizations.

The rollout process typically begins with a structured pilot phase with a few locations or a few customers. Once the pilot is successful, the idea is expanded to a larger region to test scalability and address any remaining issues. To ensure smooth adoption, these companies provide comprehensive training and support to employees. Dedicated implementation teams oversee the process, maintaining consistency and resolving challenges as they arise. This systematic approach minimizes confusion and accelerates the adoption of new practices.

Effective communication is integral to a good scaling process. By sharing test results, including clear metrics of success, it builds trust and excitement among employees, fostering alignment and enthusiasm for the changes. Throughout the initial rollout phase, the companies closely monitor performance, collect feedback, and make necessary adjustments to refine the solution before full implementation.

Use the Implementation Features of Testing Platforms

Many testing tools include functionality to simplify implementation. By leveraging these platforms, teams can push successful test changes live with minimal effort. For example, Google Ads's Drafts & Experiments feature allows advertisers to directly apply successful experiments to their live campaigns with a single click.

A standout feature of Optimizely and Visual Website Optimizer is their built-in implementation capabilities. Once an experiment shows positive results, they enable teams to roll out changes to 100 percent of users in real time without requiring developers to manually update the codebase.

LaunchDarkly is a feature management and experimentation platform that enables software development teams to control and manage feature releases efficiently. By utilizing feature flags, LaunchDarkly allows teams to toggle features on or off in real time without deploying new code, facilitating safer and more controlled rollouts.

Use AI to Increase Software Engineering Productivity

One of the biggest barriers to deploying new solutions for many companies is the bottleneck in software development. Engineers who master tools like GitHub Copilot can expect to see remarkable improvements in productivity, becoming twice as efficient at code documentation and 30–40 percent more productive at simple code generation tasks.[29]

If AI continues to improve at its current pace, the impact on software engineering will be transformative. By 2026, AI is projected to handle an even greater share of software development. According to Anthropic CEO Dario Amodei, AI models could manage up to 90 percent of software engineering tasks by then.[30] This suggests a near future where writing software code could become almost instantaneous and almost free. For growth teams, this shift will likely enable much faster implementation of complex solutions that require heavy software engineering. But the advantage will go to companies whose engineering teams quickly adopt AI coding tools and learn to use them effectively. Mastering these tools is likely to be a key competitive edge soon.

CONCLUSION

I want to share one final story with you, one that I hope inspires you as much as it inspired me. Whether you're an entrepreneur, a recent graduate, or an experienced executive, this story reinforces the core promise of this book: To grow into a towering sequoia, a company that stands far above its competition, all it takes is the courage to think differently and try new things.

MINT CONDITION FITNESS—THE GYM WITH A CLV TWENTY-EIGHT TIMES HIGHER THAN AVERAGE

As a teenager, Colin Triplett was helping clean out his late grandfather's house when he stumbled upon a list that brought him to tears. It was a catalog of his grandfather's twenty-three medications: painkillers, pills to counter their side effects, sleeping aids, stimulants to fight the resulting fatigue, and many more. In that moment, amid his grief, Colin discovered his purpose: to help others live healthier, fuller lives right up to their last day.[1]

Colin began his career as a personal fitness coach, driving from one client's home to the next. For a long time, he struggled to make ends meet in expensive Silicon Valley, earning just $30,000 a year.

Eventually, word spread about Colin's passion and knowledge and the results his clients were achieving. Soon thereafter, Colin opened Mint Condition Fitness, his own private training gym, which now generates

$1.2 million annually. Colin has recently moved to Los Angeles to open a second location and is planning many more in the future. Colin, who doesn't have a background in business, credits his success to three important principles.

Focus on the Long Term

Mint Condition Fitness isn't your typical gym that's flooded with "January joiners" who disappear by spring. Instead, Colin has designed a gym that attracts members who are serious about improving their health for the long term and are willing to make the physical, emotional, and financial investment to achieve that goal. Mint does this brilliantly using a well-honed process.

Step 1—Attract the right clients: Mint targets only clients aged fifty and above. They do this because these clients get the most benefit from health coaching, are less likely to move and abandon their membership, and have much higher average disposable income.

Step 2—Assess if the client is a right fit: Mint turns away clients they don't think they can genuinely help. As Colin says, "We only take on a new member when we are confident we can wow them and change their lives." Mint makes this decision during a unique evaluation process. Over six hours, prospective clients undergo a comprehensive health assessment, multiple personal training sessions, and some of the recovery services Mint has to offer, like red light therapy and compression therapy.

While it doesn't rely on fancy AI algorithms like some of the other examples in the book, this customer acquisition process is remarkably effective at identifying prospective members who are likely to stay with Mint for the long term. The best part?

Mint charges $400 for it, actually getting paid to find high-CLV members.

Step 3—Create a bespoke program: If Mint determines that a client is a good fit, they present a comprehensive, personalized program during an hour-long consultation. During this meeting, Mint walks through a detailed plan that makes a prospective member feel very confident they will achieve their health and wellness goals with Mint's expert guidance.

Step 4—Get a strong commitment: Only then is the client invited to become a member and shown prices for the first time. At that point, there is no sales pressure typical of a gym because Mint wants only clients who will fully commit on their own. New members who choose to join must sign a twelve-month commitment.

Step 5—Onboard clients well: While it's great to get new members to sign a twelve-month commitment, Colin wants to have an impact on each client's life, for many years. The process starts with a great onboarding process. Mint provides new members with a comprehensive sixteen-page *New Member Success Guide*. This guide outlines Mint's overarching approach, details the available technologies and services, and offers actionable suggestions to help members maximize the benefits of using Mint. Each new member then goes through a more thorough evaluation to establish a baseline on more than a hundred health and wellness metrics. New members then receive what is likely the most comprehensive health and wellness report they've seen in their lives, including an assessment of their "biological age," which measures the physiological condition of their body and is a better predictor of health risks than chronological age.

Step 6—Keep members engaged for the long term: To ensure members renew year after year, they receive a detailed monthly progress report that demonstrates clear results. As discussed previously, helping a customer generate results is more predictive of their loyalty than their satisfaction. Mint also updates each member's workout program every two weeks to ensure results are always maximized.

Another reason members stay for years is that they develop strong bonds with other members. Since most sessions are semi-private, members book workouts with people they know, which creates a sense of community and accountability—members don't want to let their group down by missing sessions or leaving the gym at renewal time.

Step 7—Increase CLV over time: Mint is always looking for ways to increase the CLV of its members. First, as members see the improvement in their lives, many upgrade to a higher pricing tier to accelerate results. Mint also continually adds new services, which create opportunities to raise prices while delivering great value to members. For example, Mint recently introduced nutrition coaching, which is now bundled into the higher membership tiers. This has increased the percentage of members in those higher tiers.

Step 8—Encourage referrals: As part of Mint's referral program, each new member receives an exclusive "Mint Coin," a physical coin that grants only one person they know a 50 percent discount on Mint's health assessment. This unique approach to referrals not only generates a steady stream of qualified leads but often attracts prospects with high CLV, similar to that of the referring member.

The results of this CLV-based strategy are incredible. While the average gym churns around 29 percent of its members a year, Mint churns less than 4 percent. Even during the pandemic, 90 percent of members stayed with Mint, working out on Zoom. And while the average gym membership fee is around $60 a month, Mint's is more than $900. A simple discounted cash flow analysis, at a 10 percent discount rate, shows that the five-year CLV of a new customer is about $1,360 for the average gym and $38,000 for Mint.

Deliver an Amazing Customer Experience

Financial success is great. As Colin says, "The more profitable we are, the more people we can help." But what's even better, and why Colin got into this business in the first place, is to change people's lives.

As of this writing, Mint Condition Fitness has 115 Google reviews, all five stars. Many include life-changing testimonials, like this one from Neelima Avadhanula: "I joined Mint in January 2024 when I hit an absolute low point in my health and fitness. Being a busy tech executive and a mother of a teenager, I had ignored my health for years. As a result, I was morbidly obese and could barely walk 100 steps without losing my breath. Over the months at Mint, my strength increased, weight dropped, and my functionality improved drastically."

Mint gets rave reviews because it has designed an amazing customer experience for its target market of older members. This customer experience includes:

Exceptional coaching: Coaching a seventy-year-old with significant health issues is far more complex than training a younger client focused on building muscle. Older clients face unique challenges, including muscle loss, declining bone density, joint stiffness, and balance issues, all of which require trainers to have a deep understanding of aging physiology.

At Mint, coaches design safe, bespoke programs that incorporate strength training to combat muscle loss, weight-bearing exercises to improve bone health, and low-impact movements to address joint pain and mobility. They also emphasize core strength, balance, and stability to reduce the risk of falls, an essential focus for older adults.

In addition to physical limitations, older clients often have chronic health conditions like heart disease, diabetes, or hypertension. Mint's trainers customize workouts to accommodate these conditions, adjusting exercise intensity, monitoring progress closely, and prioritizing safety over speed. Their expertise ensures that clients achieve measurable results without risking injury, delivering a level of care and effectiveness that sets Mint apart and is hard to copy.

To put this knowledge into practice, Mint has developed a unique system called Active Coaching, a philosophy that ensures every coach is hyperpresent during every single repetition of every session. Unlike traditional coaching, where trainers are often more focused on small talk, Active Coaching demands unwavering focus and engagement. Coaches carefully watch for proper form, breathing, and effort to ensure safety while helping clients get the most from each movement. Every correction, encouragement, or adjustment is delivered in real time, creating a level of personal attention that drives exceptional results.

One of the reasons Mint can attract the best coaches, in addition to being a mission-driven organization with great values and an exceptional culture, is that Colin pays his trainers top salaries and provides them benefits unheard of in the industry, including 401(k) matching, health benefits, guaranteed salaries even when a trainer loses a client, and paid vacation. Mint can afford these generous benefits because its CLV is twenty-eight times higher than average.

A culture of caring: Outside of workouts, the Mint Condition Fitness team goes above and beyond. When a client left their workout clothes in the changing room, one staff member took them home, washed them, and brought them to the member's home the next day. During the pandemic, when almost all home gym equipment was sold out, Mint gave their equipment to clients so they had the right equipment to train at home. When a client began showing signs of dementia and could no longer drive, Mint's general manager personally picked him up from his home twice a week and brought him to Mint to make sure he could still get his workout done.

A deeply personalized experience: In addition to personalizing workouts, Mint also personalizes the entire experience. Mint will customize music and coffee pods for gym members. And if a client mentions having a challenge at work or in their personal life, Mint may buy them a book that might help.

A tight-knit community: To cultivate a strong sense of community, which helps members achieve better results and stay with Mint longer, Mint hosts social gatherings, group hikes, charity events, and monthly guest speakers covering a wide range of topics like meditation, cooking, and sleep. Mint also encourages member interactions through its app, making it easy to coordinate semiprivate training sessions with friends.

Additionally, Mint implements creative recognition systems, such as an achievement pyramid that allows members to climb a competitive ladder based on their progress, and a Member of the Month ceremony to celebrate members who made the most progress on the pyramid.

Improve Fast

Colin is dedicated to continuously improving the outcomes of members while increasing the profitability of his business by:

- **Fostering a culture of innovation:** Every week, during the coaches' meeting, one coach presents an idea based on the latest health and wellness research. The most promising ideas are tested the following week and incorporated into Mint's system right away if they work. For example, Mint recently introduced vibration training to help members with neuropathy.

- **Committing to professional development:** Mint is one of few fitness organizations that pays for coaches to attend seminars. This commitment to professional growth enables Mint to offer its members the most advanced, evidence-based training methods available. One of the team's key learning goals next year is to deepen their understanding of neurology to better understand how the brain and body work together.

- **Leveraging cutting-edge technology:** Colin is open-minded and curious by nature. Even though he knows more about training older clients than almost anyone else, he's constantly trying new technologies to improve the results of his members. For example, Mint now uses PNOĒ and SECA testing to tailor plans for each member and track their progress. In under ten minutes, PNOĒ provides data on twenty-three biomarkers like energy levels, cellular function, heart and lung fitness, fat-burning efficiency, and biological age. SECA provides a client's muscle mass, body fat, hydration levels, inflammation, and cellular health.

  Mint is now even developing its own AI system to personalize each member's program, based on the hundreds of data points Mint collects every month from each member.

Pretty impressive, right? Here's the thing: Colin didn't do anything difficult. He just thought differently than other gym owners. He focused on the long term and created a system to maximize CLV while delighting customers. Starting with simple ideas, he made steady, incremental gains every day. Now he's using expensive, cutting-edge technologies, his business is improving at an accelerating rate, and I have no doubt he will help thousands of people lead a better life . . . and grow a much larger and much more profitable business.

PLANT THE SEED NOW

Did you know that every towering sequoia begins as a tiny seed, no bigger than a pinhead? Why not plant that seed now? Before you set this book aside, choose one simple idea from its pages and start testing it. Put the test in motion today if you can. Then test another idea. And another. Before you know it, that seed will grow into the tallest sequoia in the forest.

PAY IT FORWARD

Looking back, I wish I knew the concepts in this book earlier in my career. I would have been a more effective entrepreneur, corporate leader, and adviser. If you found this book valuable, consider sharing a copy with a young executive or an aspiring entrepreneur. This simple act of mentorship could help them transform their career. My hope is that this book helps you achieve your own aspirations but also enables you to be a catalyst for others' success.

SOURCES

Introduction

1. Invisalign stock's price increased by 18 percent after the Q4 2020 earnings announcement, leading to an increase in market capitalization of $7.1B. Invisalign's stock has since declined. Throughout the book, we'll highlight case studies of companies that may not be performing as well today as they once did. These examples are included because they provide valuable lessons.

2. SmileDirectClub Q4 2020 financial report.

3. All information about Asbury in the book comes from an interview with Miran Maric, former CMO.

4. Asbury 2014 and 2019 annual reports.

5. ConsumerShield Research Team, *How many new cars are sold each year?* (2025). ConsumerShield.

6. AutoNation 2014 and 2019 annual reports.

7. While I played a role in many of these companies' successes, it was most often the Google account teams who led the charge. They deserve the lion's share of the credit.

8. I completely agree with Steve Jobs's philosophy that creating "insanely great products" is the most important thing a company can do. However, during my time as Google's chief evangelist, my focus lay elsewhere, and for that reason, this book won't discuss how to create great products.

9. The revenue generated by an advertising investment divided by that advertising investment.

Chapter 1

1. Ehrlich, B. S., McNeil, M. J., Pham, L. T. D., Chen, Y., Rivera, J. & Acuna, C., et al. (2023). *Treatment-related mortality in children with cancer in low-income and middle-income countries: A systematic review and meta-analysis. Lancet Oncology,* 24(9), 967–977. https://doi.org/10.1016/S1470-2045(23)00318-2.

2. Shipley, K. (2021, January). *How one brand is future-proofing its mission by engaging a new generation.* Think with Google.

SOURCES

3. ChatGPT 4o answer on December 14, 2024.

4. Gemini 1.5 Pro answer on December 14, 2024.

5. Google. (2014). *EverQuote adopts a profit-driven approach for its website.* Think with Google.

6. Google. (2014, May). *Autobytel boosts profits from AdWords over 60% by putting customers in the driver's seat.* Think with Google.

7. $50 million – $5 million of extra costs – $10 million in advertising investment = $35 million profit.

8. Google's advertising AI analyzes historical transaction data shared by this retailer to identify which audiences, ads, and placements drive the highest profits. It then adjusts bids dynamically, increasing them for ads it predicts will be highly profitable and lowering them for less promising ones. Budgets are automatically reallocated to ads that are expected to deliver the maximum total profit. It's quite magical!

9. Google's advertising AI does this as described previously. In this case, transactions with items very likely to be returned will be less profitable so Google's AI will learn over time which ads for which audiences lead to lower returns.

10. Wang, E. (2024). *How Pandora unlocks incremental value all holiday season long.* Think with Google.

11. Google. (2014, August). *Why Airbnb takes a customer-centric approach to AdWords.* Think with Google.

12. Think with Google. (2024). *How Wyndham's CMO and CFO joined forces to stay budget agile* [Video]. YouTube.

13. Think with Google. (n.d.). *TAP sales take off in new international markets with Google Ads.*

14. Gulin-Merle, M. (2022). *Agility often starts with breaking down silos. Here are 3 things to get right.* Think with Google.

15. Gulin-Merle, M. (2022).

16. Darveau-Garneau, N.& Deif, A. (2018). *5 rules for winning with automated marketing.* Think with Google.

17. Statsig. (2024, April 16). *PLG: 4 case studies to learn.*

18. For more on testing using profit instead of conversion, read: Polonioli, A. (2022). *Does great conversion rate optimization guarantee profitability?* Coveo.

19. Bryan, C. (2016, March 30). *The business case for integrated demand generation: How B2B marketers deliver measurable results—elevating their companies and their careers.* Eloqua.

20. Purde, A. (2022, October 2). *Lead scoring: The complete guide for B2B sales and marketing—2023 update.* Outfunnel.

SOURCES

21. I personally find it hard to believe that number. *Integrated Care Journal*. (2024). *NHS procurement criteria set for major changes*. Integrated Care Journal.

22. Keller, S. (2017). *Attracting and retaining the right talent*. McKinsey & Company.

23. Culture Amp. (2024). *How PwC uses data to retain high-performing employees*.

Chapter 2

1. Schwab, P.-N. (2024). *American Airlines got rid of its most loyal customer*. IntoTheMinds.

2. Bernstein Research. (2022). *HelloFresh: Paying people to eat*. Alliance Bernstein.

3. Hoyne, N. (2022). *Converted: The data-driven way to win customers' hearts*. Portfolio.

4. Luck, I. (2023, May 31). *5 innovative customer retention examples and case studies*. CustomerGauge.

5. Jain, A. (2023, May 5). *Customer lifetime value (CLV): A critical metric for building strong customer relationships*. Gartner Digital Markets.

6. Cvetanovski, B., Hazan, E., Perrey, J. & Spillecke, D. (2019, September 26). *Are you a growth leader? The seven beliefs and behaviors that growth leaders share*. McKinsey & Company.

7. Cvetanovski, B., Hazan, E., Perrey, J. & Spillecke, D. (2019, September 26).

8. For more on why many companies don't make decisions using imperfect data, read professional poker player Annie Duke's excellent book, *Thinking in Bets*. Duke, A. (2018). *Thinking in bets: Making smarter decisions when you don't have all the facts*. Portfolio/Penguin.

9. Statista. (2024). *Apple worldwide shipments of smartphones from 2010 to 2024, by quarter (in million units)*. Statista.

10. Leswing, K. (2023, August 3). *Apple's most profitable line of business is making up for some hardware struggles*. CNBC.

11. Counterpoint. (2019, September 16). *Apple iPhone & Apple Watch price drop—A strategic masterstroke!* Counterpoint Research.

12. 35 percent margin on a $1,000 phone and 70 percent margin on $1,400 of services.

13. $700 for an iPhone 11 at a 35 percent margin.

14. Richter, W. (2021). *Today's unicorns have bigger cumulative losses than Amazon, had lost money far longer than Amazon, still don't show a turnaround*. Wolf Street.

15. Fader, P. & Hoyne, N. (2021). *Important lessons for embracing customer lifetime value*. Think with Google.

16. Spanier, J. (2019, November). *Inside Google Marketing: 3 marketing myths we busted this past year*. Think with Google.

17. McCarthy, D. & Fader, P. (2020). *How to value a company by analyzing its customers. Harvard Business Review.*

18. Maksymovych, O. (2019, April 15). *Ocado: Significant results thanks to big data.* Cloudfresh.

19. Genter, J. T. (2018, January 8). *American Airlines' secret passenger scoring system revealed.* The Points Guy.

20. Amazon Stories EU. (2024). *Amazon's Prime delivery speeds are faster than ever so far in 2024* [Video]. YouTube.

21. Walker, S. M. (2024). *PR/FAQ: The Amazon working backwards framework for product innovation (2024).* Product Strategy.

22. Agrawal, A., Gans, J. S. & Goldfarb, A. (2018). *Prediction machines: The simple economics of artificial intelligence.* Harvard Business Review Press.

23. Siegel, E. (2013). *Predictive analytics: The power to predict who will click, buy, lie, or die.* Wiley.

24. Kammerlander, C., Kolb, V., Luegmair, M., Scheermann, L., Schmailzl, M., Seufert, M., Zhang, J., Dalic, D. & Schön, T. (2025). *Machine learning models for soil parameter prediction based on satellite, weather, clay and yield data.* arXiv.

25. Heuritech. (n.d.). *How to achieve +9% in sales in the skirts category?* Heuritech.

26. Source: Tractable.

27. Reynolds, S. (2025, February 26). *Can AI help predict which cancer patients should be treated with immunotherapy?* National Cancer Institute.

28. Source: Geotab.

29. Nearing, G., Cohen, D., Dube, V., Gauch, M., Gilon, O., Harrigan, S., Hassidim, A., Klotz, D., Kratzert, F., Metzger, A., Nevo, S., Pappenberger, F., Prudhomme, C., Shalev, G., Shenzis, S., Tekalign, T. Y., Weitzner, D. & Matias, Y. (2024). *Global prediction of extreme floods in ungauged watersheds. Nature, 627*(559–563).

30. Temperton, J. (2016, July 7). *Beer brewed with AI? Yup, that's now a thing.* WIRED.

Chapter 3

1. Packer, G. (2014, February 9). *Cheap words. New Yorker.*

2. Vaziri, S. (2024, February 15). *Typical car accident settlement amounts in California.* Vaziri Law Group.

3. Disclosure: As of this writing, I am advising Surex's parent company, IA Financial. I was a former member of the board of directors of the company and have equity in the company.

4. Iketani, S., Imai, A., Takahashi, T. & Kondo, N. (2019). *How IDOM tailored its campaigns to reach high-value car buyers in Japan.* Think with Google.

5. Roth, J. (2019). *How turning to automation helped one company drive profitable growth.* Think with Google.

6. Baekholm, D. (2018). *Want to deliver great customer experiences? Here's what not to do.* Think with Google.

7. Mortensen, A. (2024). *Win more high-value customers and drive sustainable growth.* Think with Google.

8. Adams, L. & Taylor, D. (2024, November). *Unlocking the 80/20 rule: How to build customer lifetime value.* Think with Google.

9. Takahashi, D. (2014, February 26). *Only 0.15 percent of mobile gamers account for 50 percent of all in-game revenue (exclusive).* GamesBeat.

10. Navot, Y. (n.d.). *Identifying your most valuable customer segments.* XP^2 Personalization & Targeting Course, Dynamic Yield.

11. Navot, Y. (n.d.).

12. ChatGPT 4o model, prompted December 14, 2024. As always, be sure to double-check anything Large Language Models say.

13. Reinartz, W. J. & Kumar, V. (2002). *The mismanagement of customer loyalty.* Harvard Business Review.

14. Noone, B. & Griffin, P. (1999). *Managing the long-term profit yield from market segments in a hotel environment: a case study on the implementation of customer profitability analysis.* International Journal of Hospitality Management, 18, 111–128.

15. Lawson, M. & Grudnowski, J. (2017, June). *Ignite growth by rallying your organization around a customer-first mindset.* Think with Google.

16. Eggert, A., Steinhoff, L. & Witte, C. (2019). *Gift purchases as catalysts for strengthening customer–brand relationships.* Journal of Marketing, 83(5), 115–132.

17. Google + Material Business Value of Apps research study, US, app users ($n = 2,406$), app non-users ($n = 2,404$), November 2022–January 2023.

18. Paytronix. (2024). *Online ordering report 2024.*

19. Artificial Intelligence Act. (2023). *European Artificial Intelligence Act.* European Union.

20. Sato, K. (2017). *Using machine learning for insurance pricing optimization.* Google Cloud.

21. Mankowitz, D. J., Michi, A., Zhernov, A., Gelmi, M., Selvi, M., Paduraru, C., Leurent, E., Iqbal, S., Lespiau, J.-B., Ahern, A., Köppe, T., Millikin, K., Gaffney, S., Elster, S., . . . & Silver, D. (2023). *Faster sorting algorithms discovered using deep reinforcement learning.* Nature, 618(257–263).

22. Progressive. (2023, Q4). *Investor relations: Destination Era and Progressive Advantage Agency.*

23. Kumar, S. & Pandey, M. (2017). *The impact of psychological pricing strategy on consumers' buying behaviour: A qualitative study. International Journal of Business and Systems Research*, 11(1/2), 101.

24. Lee, R. (2021). *The secret to long-term consumer-tech success: Subscription pricing. Forbes.*

25. Statt, N. (2019). *Why MoviePass really failed: An industry-shaking idea, and a company that flew directly into the sun. The Verge.*

26. Careless, J. (2021). *Dynamic pricing benefits attractions.* IAAPA.

27. OpenView Venture Partners. (n.d.). *Usage-based pricing: The next evolution in software pricing.*

28. Zhang, X., Phan, T. Q. & Yang, A. X. (2019). *Grandfather clause and customer loyalty: Evidence from a quasi-experiment.* SSRN.

29. Nagle, T. T., Hogan, J. E. & Zale, J. (2010). *The strategy and tactics of pricing: A guide to growing more profitably* (5th ed.). Pearson.

30. Kakas, A. (2024). *Dynamic pricing: Balancing profit and customer satisfaction.* LinkedIn.

31. Ellis, S. & Brown, M. (2017). *Hacking growth: How today's fastest-growing companies drive breakout success.* Currency.

32. Hoffman, R. & Yeh, C. (2018). *Blitzscaling: The lightning-fast path to building massively valuable companies.* Currency.

33. Karapetyan, S. (2023). *7 growth hacking examples to steal for your strategy.* The Product Manager.

Chapter 4

1. Autry, A. (2021, June 1). *Loyalty statistics: The ultimate collection.* Access.

2. Chahal, M. (2014, June 4). *The challenges of customer lifetime value. Marketing Week.*

3. Progressive. (2023, Q4). *Investor relations: Destination Era and Progressive Advantage Agency.*

4. Moy, P. (2017). *Not just for newbies: Use digital to nurture your existing high-value customers.* Think with Google.

5. Darveau-Garneau, N. & Deif, A. (2018, November). *5 rules for winning with automated marketing.* Think with Google.

6. McKinnon, T. (2023). *Target's eCommerce strategy: Why it's outperforming.* Indigo Digital.

7. Markey, R. (2020, January–February). *Are you undervaluing your customers? Harvard Business Review.*

8. McCarthy, D., Fader, P. & Hardie, B. (2016). *V(CLV): Examining Variance in Models of Customer Lifetime Value.* The Wharton School.

9. Userpilot. (2024). *What is a customer churn prediction & how to set it up.*

SOURCES

10. Blue Orange. (n.d.). *3 best machine learning models to predict customer lifetime value (CLTV)*.

11. Banu, J., Neelakandan, S., Geetha, B., Selvalakshmi, V., Umadevi, A. & Martinson, E. (2022). *Artificial Intelligence Based Customer Churn Prediction Model for Business Markets*. Computational Intelligence and Neuroscience.

12. Curiskis, S., Dong, X., Jiang, F. & Scarr, M. (2023). *A novel approach to predicting customer lifetime value in B2B SaaS companies*. *Journal of Marketing Analytics*, 11(587–601).

13. Cowan, G., Mercuri, S. & Khraishi, R. (2023). *Modelling customer lifetime-value in the retail banking industry*. arXiv.

14. Janakiraman, A. (2023, September 14). *Expedia Group's customer lifetime value prediction model: Understanding customer behavior for profitability*. Expedia Group Technology. Medium.

15. Venkatesan, R. & Kumar, V. (2004). *A customer lifetime value framework for customer selection and resource allocation strategy*. *Journal of Marketing*, 68, 106–125.

16. Fader, P. & Toms, S. E. (2018). *The customer centricity playbook: Implement a winning strategy driven by customer lifetime value*. Wharton School Press.

17. Fader, P. & Toms, S. E. (2018).

18. Shah, D. & Kumar, V. (2012, December). *The dark side of cross-selling*. *Harvard Business Review*.

19. Campaign. (n.d.). *How EasyJet transformed customer data into emotional anniversary stories*. Campaign.

20. Mittal, V., Sarkees, M. & Murshed, F. (2008, April). *The right way to manage unprofitable customers*. *Harvard Business Review*.

21. Abraham, M., Van Kerckhove, J.-F., Archacki, R., Esteve González, J. & Fanfarillo, S. (2019, June). *The next level of retail personalization*. Boston Consulting Group.

22. Brooks, A., McArdle, L. & Friedlander, M. (2024). *The best home and auto insurance bundles of 2024: Bundling your home and auto coverage may save you money and simplify your policy management*. Bankrate.

23. Backlinko Team. (2024). *Amazon Prime user and revenue statistics*. Backlinko.

24. Miller, A. (2023, June 21). *Uncovering America's Amazon obsession, state by state [2023 data survey]*. Upgraded Points.

25. Mattioli, D. (2024). *Alexa is in millions of households—and Amazon is losing billions*. *Wall Street Journal*.

26. Kim, E. (2018, January 3). *Amazon Echo owners spend more on Amazon than Prime members, report says*. CNBC.

27. Mattioli, D. (2024). *Alexa is in millions of households—and Amazon is losing billions*. *Wall Street Journal*.

28. Backlinko Team. (2024). *Amazon Prime user and revenue statistics*. Backlinko.

29. CapitalOne Shopping Research. (2024). *Amazon logistics statistics*.

30. Vasudev, A. (2021). *How Zappos "Delivers happiness to soles and souls."* The Strategy Story and Petersen, R. (2017). *9 inspiring case studies of customer lifetime value (CLV)*. BarnRaisers.

31. Liedtke, M. (2024). *20 years ago, people thought Google's Gmail launch was an April Fool's Day joke*. PBS News.

Chapter 5

1. Bauer, T., Boudet, J., Lamb, M. & Robinson, K. (2020, June 15). *Performance branding and how it is reinventing marketing ROI*. McKinsey & Company.

2. Hollis, N. (2013, October 25). *Marketing's mission: Make it meaningfully different*. Harvard Business Review.

3. Mirzaei, A., Baumann, C., Johnson, L. W. & Gray, D. (2016). *The impact of brand health on customer equity*. Journal of Retailing and Consumer Services, 33, 8–16. https://doi.org/10.1016/j.jretconser.2016.07.002.

4. Shapiro, B. T., Hitsch, G. J., & Tuchman, A. E. (2021). *TV advertising effectiveness and profitability: Generalizable results from 288 brands*. Econometrica., 89(4), 1855–1879.

5. Invisalign's stock price increased by 18 percent after the Q4 2020 earnings announcement, leading to an increase in market capitalization of $7.1B. SmileDirectClub's stock price declined.

6. Interview with Cecelia Wogan-Silva.

7. Bhandal, K. & Heydt, S. (2021, April). *Navigating a new partnership and the pandemic: What Align Technology and Publicis Groupe learned*. Think with Google.

8. Interview with Cecelia Wogan-Silva.

9. Bhandal, K. & Heydt, S. (2021, April).

10. Darveau-Garneau, N. (2020, March). *Reach beyond reach: Brand marketing in the age of machine learning*. Think with Google.

11. CSI. (2024, September 5). *US pay-TV loses 1.62M subs in Q2'24. CSI Magazine*.

12. Hartman, K. (2019, June). *How to bring your marketing mix modeling into the 21st century*. Think with Google.

13. Nielsen NPower and Nielsen Ad Intel for the month of October 2020.

14. Google Marketing tests 2019–2021, Nielsen measured.

15. Thomaz, F., Bell, J. & Stephen, A. (n.d.). *No silver bullet: Finding the right recipe for effective brand advertising*. University of Oxford, Saïd Business School, Oxford Future of Marketing Initiative & Kantar.

SOURCES

16. According to a Nielsen Total Ad Ratings Meta-Analysis from 2019, on average, heavy TV viewers see an ad 26.5 times, whereas on YouTube the average frequency is 2.6 times.

17. Eye square GmbH, April 2021, *Comparing YouTube and TV* custom study.

18. Google search lift meta-analysis, US 2018.

19. Nielsen MMM Meta-Analysis, US 2017–2018.

20. Nash, M. (2024, February). *What we learned when we challenged our own video marketing formula*. Think with Google.

21. Marketing Charts. (2021, May 12). *The state of traditional TV: Updated with Q3 2020 data*. Marketing Charts.

22. *CSI*. (2024, September 5).

23. Caron, P. (2023). *How Quebec City's marketing team pivoted during the pandemic and boosted hotel occupancy rates*. Think with Google.

24. Think with Google. (2022). *How a YouTube-first approach helped Mark's shift brand perception and reach new audiences*.

25. Shipley, K. (2019). *Favorite show or 40-minute ad? How one media brand blurred the lines of traditional advertising*. Think with Google.

26. L'Oréal Canada. (2023, June). *How L'Oréal Canada drives results with YouTube on connected TV* [Video]. Think with Google.

27. Gevelber, L. (2015). *Why consumer intent is more powerful than demographics*. Think with Google and Think With Google (2018). *Turn attention into action: YouTube marketing effectiveness guide*.

28. Fliegelman, O. (2018). *Your true audience may be bigger than you realize—and video could help you find out*. Think with Google.

29. Goodwin, D. (2021). *Case study: How Google Ads life events targeting lifts brand interest 175%*. WordStream by LocaliQ.

30. Google. (n.d.). *Experiment: How Airbnb sparked travelers' interest across their planning stages*. Experiment with Google Ads.

31. Puribhat, K. (2019). *How Minute Maid achieved lower funnel results by moving beyond demographics*. Think with Google.

32. Tsai, Y.-L. & Honka, E. (2018). *Non-informational advertising informing consumers: How advertising affects consumers' decision-making in the U.S. auto insurance industry*. *SSRN Electronic Journal*. https://doi.org/10.2139/ssrn.3094448.

33. Lacrampe, C. & Frerot, C. (2020). *Warner Bros. France booste la considération pour son film Tenet*. Think with Google.

SOURCES

34. Honka, Elisabeth, Ali Hortaçsu & Maria Ana Vitorino. *Advertising, consumer awareness, and choice: Evidence from the U.S. banking industry. RAND Journal of Economics* 48, no. 3 (2017): 611–646.

35. Lacrampe, C. & Frerot, C. (2020).

36. Shipley, K. (2019, June). *How one brand tackled an enduring marketing challenge: Measuring a campaign's bottom-line impact.* Think with Google.

37. Interview with Avinash Kaushik.

38. Nielsen. (2017, October). *When it comes to advertising effectiveness, what is key?* Nielsen Insights.

39. Odell, P. (2017, October 10). *When revenue flatlined, St. Jude turned it around with research.* Chief Marketer.

40. Nelson-Bogle, A. M. (2024, June). *We used AI to analyze over 8,000 top ads. Here's what we learned.* Think with Google.

41. Blankstein, J. (2023, March). *How 3 often overlooked best practices can supercharge your creative.* Think with Google.

42. Le Port, A. (2022, April). *Understanding the ABCDs of effective creative on YouTube.* Think with Google.

43. Bailey, M. (2024, September). *Inside Google marketing: How we're using AI.* Think with Google.

44. Caligiuri, C. & Jones, B. (2019). *When it comes to video ad creative, how much should you customize?* Think with Google.

45. YouTube Advertisers. (n.d.). *B&H | Success Story | YouTube Advertisers* [Video]. YouTube.

46. Accenture. (2024, August 29). *Accenture and Google Cloud advance AI adoption and cybersecurity with Fortune 500 companies.*

47. Reisman, K. (2024). *IBM reimagines content creation and digital marketing with Adobe Firefly generative AI. Adobe Experience Cloud Blog.*

48. Bailey, M. (2024, September).

49. For more information on YouTube's latest AI branding optimization tools, watch https://bit.ly/4fY9abe.

50. Nelson-Bogle, A. M. (2023). *How AI helps video marketers move at the speed of culture.* Think with Google.

51. Paterson, A. & Siddiqui, F. (2021). *How an auto brand used a video-first strategy to tell customers 7 different stories.* Think with Google.

52. Wolfe, J. (2024, June 24). *Recognizing ROI in influencer marketing: Growth, trends and challenges.* NAB Amplify.

53. Nash, M. (2024, February). *What we learned when we challenged our own video marketing formula*. Think with Google.

54. Coffee, P. (2014, June 25). *Q&A: How can brands best market to millennials? Adweek*.

55. Edelman. (2019, January 20). *2019 Edelman Trust Barometer*. Edelman.

56. Beichert, M., Bayerl, A., Goldenberg, J. & Lanz, A. (2024, February 20). *Why smaller influencers offer better marketing ROI [Research insights]*. American Marketing Association.

57. Sponsorable. (2024). *BetterHelp podcast sponsorships*.

58. Haidt, J. (2024). *The anxious generation: How the great rewiring of childhood is causing an epidemic of mental illness*. Penguin Press.

59. Blumenstein, H. & O'Neil-Hart, C. (2015, December). *How YouTube extends the reach and engagement of your video advertising*. Think with Google.

60. MacGregor, K. (2019, November). *Total Ad Ratings reveal YouTube reaches what TV misses*. Think with Google.

61. Tuchtenhagen, J. (2019, July). *Inside Google marketing: How we think about digital-first planning*. Think with Google.

62. Fliegelman, O. (2018, August). *3 lessons from the U.S. Navy's first made-for-digital video recruitment campaign*. Think with Google.

63. Think with Google. (2013, August). *How Travel Oklahoma is bucking tradition to win visitors*. Think with Google.

64. Schawbel, D. (2023). *Airbnb CMO ditches performance for bold brand campaigns*. Personal Branding Blog.

65. Fitzgerald, K. (2020). *Think video marketing doesn't include performance marketing? Think again*. Think with Google.

Chapter 6

1. Salesforce Research. (2020). *State of the connected customer: 4th edition* and Salesforce Research. (2022). *State of the connected customer: 5th edition*.

2. PwC. (n.d.). *Experience is everything: Here's how to do it*. PwC.

3. Accenture. (2017). *B2B Customer Experience 2017*.

4. Bough, V., Ehrlich, O., Fanderl, H. & Schiff, R. (2023). *Experience-led growth: A new way to create value*. McKinsey & Company.

5. Forrester Customer Experience Index 2022.

6. Bain & Company. (2022). *Customer Behavior and Loyalty in Retail Banking*.

7. ACSI Retail Report 2022.

SOURCES

8. Capgemini Research Institute. (2025). *World Life Insurance report 2025: Bridge the customer experience divide: Ensure life insurance relevancy through relentless customer centricity*. Capgemini.

9. Gartner. (2021). *Customer experience benchmarks.*

10. Deloitte Digital Transformation Survey 2022.

11. Hall, B., Lamarre, E., Levin, R., Lorenz, J.-T. & Simon, P. (2024, January 12). *Rewired and ahead: Digital and AI leaders are leaving the rest behind.* McKinsey Digital.

12. Hall, B., Lamarre, E., Levin, R., Lorenz, J.-T. & Simon, P. (2024, January 12).

13. PwC. (n.d.).

14. Gocheva, C. (2023). *NPS Financial Services / 27 Banking NPS Scores 2023.* Experience Benchmarks.

15. Andrews, L. (2024, April 7). *First Direct: Inside the firm that gets customer service right.* The Times.

16. KPMG. (2023). *Spotlight on first direct: Ranked 1st in 2023.* KPMG.

17. Deloitte Digital. (n.d.). *Personalising the customer experience.* Deloitte Digital.

18. Shirer, M. (2023, November 1). *Worldwide digital transformation spending to maintain growth trajectory, according to IDC.* IDC.

19. Bughin, J., Deakin, J. & O'Beirne, B. (2019, October 22). *Digital transformation: Improving the odds of success.* McKinsey Digital.

20. Short, E., Sauro, J. & Lewis, J. (2023, October 31). *UX and NPS benchmarks of hotel websites (2023).* MeasuringU.

21. Starbucks quarterly report Q3 2024.

22. Dixon, M., Toman, N. & Delisi, R. (2013). *The effortless experience: Conquering the new battleground for customer loyalty.* Portfolio.

23. Soundararajan, K. (2024, July 22). *Using customer bonding to maximize customer lifetime value.* Rocketlane.

24. Dutton, N. (2025, February). *Very Group finds its "bullseye" buyer by unlocking customer data.* Think with Google.

25. Milnes, H. (2016, January 6). *Inside Sephora's innovation lab.* Digiday.

26. O'Connor, B. (2023, February 23). *How Airbnb used Snow White to create raving customers: Their unique customer experiences grew them to $8.4B.* Outlier Growth.

27. Disclosure: As of this writing, I'm on the board of Alida and hold stock options.

28. Medallia & Adobe. (n.d.). *DICK'S streamlines its eCommerce experience.* Adobe Partner Story.

29. Crandell, C. (2016, June 10). *Customer co-creation is the secret sauce to success. Forbes.*

30. Braineet. (n.d.). *Customer co-creation examples: 12 companies doing it right.*

SOURCES

31. Li, J., Hudson, S. & So, K. K. F. (2019). *Exploring the customer experience with Airbnb. International Journal of Culture, Tourism and Hospitality Research*, 13(4), 458–471.

32. Diebner, R., Malfara, D., Neher, K., Thompson, M. & Vancauwenberghe, M. (2021, February). *Prediction: The future of CX*. McKinsey & Company.

33. Schaeffer, C. (2017, June 9). *How to design your 360-degree customer view*. CustomerThink.

34. Dias, J., Ionuțiu, O., Lhuer, X. & van Ouwerkerk, J. (2016). *The four pillars of distinctive customer journeys*. McKinsey & Company.

35. PwC. (n.d.).

36. Hall, B., Lamarre, E., Levin, R., Lorenz, J.-T. & Simon, P. (2024, January 12).

37. Chen, O. (2024, December 3). *How GiveDirectly increased donations by over $3 million/ year through experimentation. Lenny's Newsletter*.

38. Bitca, A. (2024). *Three main causes of customer churn*. Retently.

39. The Good. (2023, June 20). *11 examples of the best onboarding experiences in SaaS to inspire your own*. Medium.

40. Hayes, A. (2024, June 25). *8 stats that prove the power of app demo videos*. Wyzowl.

41. The Good. (2023, June 20).

42. Verstegen, C. (2024, July 10). *ZoomInfo's award-winning customer onboarding initiatives*. ZoomInfo.

43. Juviler, J. (2022, April 11). *19 stats that make the case for mobile optimization on your website*. HubSpot.

44. PWAStats.com: PWA case studies.

45. Schaal, D. (2010, December 21). *Hotel Tonight claims to be fastest hotel booking service*. PhocusWire.

46. There's an obvious downside to this technology. I'm not making a value judgment; I'm only reporting the facts.

47. Wilkinson, P. (2019, July 12). *Contactless collection plate tried out at York. Church Times*.

48. Heath, N. (2010, November 1). *Expedia on how one extra data field can cost $12m*. ZDNet.

49. Oxley, M. (2021, April 9). *Your eCommerce site has a conversion problem (and it's because of your UX design)*. Core dna.

50. Gartner. (n.d.). *B2B buying: How top CSOs and CMOs optimize the journey*. Gartner.

51. Navot, Y. (n.d.). *It's personal—Why it's time to deflate the great gated content debate*. XP² by Dynamic Yield.

52. Mortensen, A. (2024, October). *Win more high-value customers and drive sustainable growth*. Think with Google.

53. Abraham, M., Van Kerckhove, J.-F., Archacki, R., Esteve González, J. & Fanfarillo, S. (2019, June). *The next level of retail personalization*. Boston Consulting Group.

54. Salesforce. (n.d.). *State of the AI connected customer (7th ed.)*.

55. McKinsey. *How B2B companies win with personalization*.

56. Conversion. (n.d.). *Sport Chek case study*.

57. Balkhi, S. (2020, January 20). *5 can't-miss e-commerce personalization ideas*. *Entrepreneur*.

58. Patel, N. (n.d.). *100 conversion optimization case studies*. Neil Patel.

59. Lawson, M. (2015, September). *Win every micro-moment with a better mobile strategy*. Think with Google.

60. Govil, A. (2016, September). *Boosting app installs with real-time, data-driven creative for Waze*. Think with Google.

61. Carpio, H. (n.d.). *Dynamic personalization drives +80% ACV*. Mutiny.

62. Diebner, R., Malfara, D., Neher, K., Thompson, M. & Vancauwenberghe, M. (2021, February). *Prediction: The future of CX*. McKinsey & Company.

63. Tessitore, S. (2023, February 28). *How Wajax discovered promoters are worth 2X more than detractors*. CustomerGauge.

64. Ko, N. (n.d.). *Breaking 360: It's time to move beyond the 360-degree view of the customer*. The Future of Commerce.

65. Google Cloud. (n.d.). *American Eagle: Building a multi-terabyte marketing data warehouse* [Video]. YouTube.

66. Bawcom, A., Fitzpatrick, M., Cheung, C. W., Collins, D. & Gabrielli, D. (2024, December 9). *AI for IT modernization: Faster, cheaper, better*. McKinsey & Company.

67. Strickler, J. (2020, August 7). *Blue River Technology uses Facebook AI for weed control*. *Forbes*.

68. Interview with Marin Maric, former CMO of Asbury.

Chapter 7

1. Jerenz, A., Storozhev, A., D'Aversa, L., Boksha, N., Khan, N., Jogani, R. & Ivanov, A. (2021, November 27). *How high performers optimize IT productivity for revenue growth: A leader's guide*. McKinsey Digital.

2. Diamandis, P. (2016, April 10). *Culture & experimentation—with Uber's chief product officer*. Medium.

3. Diamandis, P. (2016, April 28). *How X (Google) experiments*. *HuffPost*.

4. ($6 profit per movie ticket sold minus $0.50 per theater visit) × 5 million movie visits.

5. Croxen-John, D. (2023, January 23). *The surprising truth about Amazon and Booking.com's culture of experimentation*. AWA.

SOURCES

6. This article explains how a design company uses AI to improve its product design process: Marion, T. J., Srour, M. & Piller, F. (2024, July 29). *When generative AI meets product development. MIT Sloan Management Review.*

7. Reichheld, F. F. & Markey, R. (2011). *The ultimate question 2.0: How net promoter companies thrive in a customer-driven world.* Harvard Business Review Press.

8. While this is beyond the scope of this book, make sure you have clear policies and governance structures in place as you deploy AI systems to mitigate against copyright issues, hallucinations, and other potential AI risks.

9. Chasinov, N. (2024, May 23). *Airbnb's North Star Metric: Explained.* Teknicks.

10. Longe, T. (2023, November 5). *North Star Metric examples from tech giants.* UXCam.

11. Russell, M. (2024, September 18). *23 powerful examples of North Star metrics that drive growth and success.* MemberSpace.

12. Progressive. (2023, Q4). *Investor relations: Destination Era and Progressive Advantage Agency.*

13. Longe, T. (2023, November 5). *North Star Metric examples from tech giants.* UXCam.

14. Wang, B. (2024, January 19). *How will SpaceX bring the cost to space down to $10 per kilogram from over $1000 per kilogram?* NextBigFuture.

15. Venditti, B. (2022, January 27). *The cost of space flight before and after SpaceX.* Visual Capitalist.

16. Wall, M. (2022, March 23). *SpaceX raises launch and Starlink prices, citing inflation.* Space.com.

17. Sesnic, T. (2024, January 11). *How does ULA's Vulcan compare to the competition?* Everyday Astronaut.

18. Benzinga. (2023, December 6). *Elon Musk says SpaceX on track to launch 80% of Earth's payloads in 2023, dominating competitors.* MooMoo.

19. Venditti, B. (2022, January 27). *The cost of space flight before and after SpaceX.* Visual Capitalist.

20. LVMH. (2024, May 23). *LVMH takes Viva Technology 2024 visitors into its dream garden.*

21. For more on testing best practices, read: Biebuyck, J. (2024, May). *The Experiments Playbook: How to run high-quality marketing experiments.* Think with Google.

22. Chen, O. (2024). *How GiveDirectly increased donations by over $3 million/year through experimentation. Lenny's Newsletter.*

23. Intuit. (n.d.). *Rapid experimentation to deliver customer benefits. Intuit Blog.*

24. Movsisyan, A. (n.d.). *How Dropbox's MVP explainer video helped it dominate the market.* Yans Media.

25. Chen, O. (2024).

26. Edelman, D. C. & Abraham, M. (2022). *Customer experience in the age of AI: The case for building "intelligent experience engines." Harvard Business Review.*

27. Abrams, A. (2024, November 7). *Breaking the rules of growth: Why Shopify bans KPIs, optimizes for churn, prioritizes intuition, and builds toward a 100-year vision* [Audio podcast episode]. *Lenny's Podcast.*

28. *The Verge.* (2019). *Airbnb Experiences: Launching with a Focus.*

29. Pandey, R., Singh, P., Wei, R. & Shankar, S. (2024). *Transforming software development: Evaluating the efficiency and challenges of GitHub Copilot in real-world projects.* arXiv. https://doi.org/10.48550/arXiv.2406.17910.

30. Kim, T. (2024, November 13). *AI agents are coming to take away your busy work. Barron's.*

Conclusion

1. If you're interested in learning more about living a healthier, fuller life, read: Attia, P. & Gifford, B. (2023). *Outlive: The science and art of longevity.* Harmony.

INDEX

Page numbers followed by *f* refer to figures.

THANK-YOUS

The wonderful team at HarperCollins and Neuwirth: Tim Burgard, Jeff Farr, and David McNeill.

My agent, James Levine, and his great team.

The Google evangelists: Alan Eagle, Neil Hoyne, Aprajita Jain, Gopi Kallayil, Cliff Redeker, Cecelia Wogan-Silva, Mike Yapp, and more than a hundred others that were Google evangelists during their careers.

The following people who generously agreed to lengthy interviews: Rob Buchanan, Heela Goonen, Neil Hoyne, Aprajita Jain, Gopi Kallayil, Avinash Kaushik, Luc Levesque, Jasper Malcolmson, Miran Maric, Nick Meads, Estelle Metayer, Lance Miller, Chris O'Neill, Rick Shadyac, Colin Triplett, Seth van der Swaagh, and Cecilia Wogan-Silva.

The following people who played an important part in developing some of the ideas in this book: Brian Albert, Michelle Allen, Angie Barrick, Don Batsford, Cyrus Behzadi, Mike Bergmann, Tomas Bodin, Natalia Böhm, Andrew Botros, Stacy Byrne, Sydney Caine, Kaitlyn Cashman, Nico Celedon, Alex Chinien, Rachelle Considine, Caroline Dillon, Jennifer Duddy, Alan Eagle, Andrew Eell, Andres Egoavil, Andrew Eifell, Spencer Einbund, Michael Falkenburgh, Ben Finkelstein, Adam Fish, Lane Fortinberry, Nicole Franz, Kevin Fried, Lauren Garcia, Lissette Gole, Ernst Hagen, Pashmeena Hilal, Vicky Homan, Ryan Hornacek, Neil Hoyne, Aprajita Jain, Anita Joseph, Gopi Kallayil, Suesan Katz, Avinash Kaushik, Sarah Kelaita, Neil Kirby, Leonard Kongshavn, Justyna Kujtkowska, Anurag Kumar, Bill Lan, Matthew Lawson, Jim Lecinski, Philip Lenhoff, Luc Levesque, Tara Walpert Levy, Jasper Malcolmson,

Bey Mao, Miran Maric, Axel Mathysen Gerst, Paul McConnell, Julie McKernan, Matt McMahon, Helen Mooney, Erin Moran, Daniel Morgan, Eric Morris, Jordan Neidig, Shawn Pao, Sonal Patel, Molly Quinn, Cliff Redeker, Elyse Riddington, Sudeep Roy, Greg Schaffer, Marissa Seastrand, Lucy Seery, Jason Shirk, Emily Smith, Eric Spamer, Adam Stewart, Joshua Stuebing, Vivian Sullivan, Jeff Sundheim, Sarah Thomas, Diarmid Thomson, Emily Waskevich, Don Wilson, Robin Wiman, Cecelia Wogan-Silva, and Mike Yapp.

ABOUT THE AUTHOR

NICOLAS DARVEAU-GARNEAU is an AI and digital transformation expert with more than twenty-five years of experience. As Google's chief evangelist, Nicolas worked with the C-suites of more than a thousand of Google's top customers to help them accelerate their digital transformation. He also worked as chief strategy and growth officer at Coveo, a leading AI company. He currently serves on the boards of the Toronto Stock Exchange, McEwen Mining, and Alida. He is a sought-after speaker and consultant.